nothing to it

BROTHER PHAP HAI

nothing to it

ten ways to be at home with yourself

PARALLAX
PRESS
Berkeley, California

Parallax Press
P.O. Box 7355
Berkeley, California 94707
parallax.org

Parallax Press is the publishing division of Unified Buddhist Church
© 2015 Unified Buddhist Church
All rights reserved
Printed in The United States of America

Cover and text design by Jess Morphew
Cover illustrations: couch, Giorgio Morara/istock;
cat, Jonah Wong/Shutterstock
Author Photo © Ron Forster
Interior illustration: Magnia/Shutterstock

Unless otherwise noted, foreign terms that appear throughout the text
are in Pali, except in the case of Mahayana sutras and references to
Buddhist Psychology, when the terms are in Sanskrit. Pali and Sanskrit
have been transliterated informally, without the diacritical marks. The
"s" has been written "sh" when it is pronounced that way. The Pali and
other foreign terms have been italicized the first time they appear, and
definitions are provided at that time.

Library of Congress Cataloging-in-Publication Data

Phap Hai, Brother, author.
 Nothing to it : ten ways to be at home with yourself / Brother Phap
Hai.
    pages cm
 ISBN 978-1-941529-00-3 (paperback)
 1. Spiritual life–Buddhism. I. Title.
 BQ5660.P43 2015
 294.3'444–dc23
                                             2015027489

ISBN 978-1-941529-00-3

1 2 3 4 5 / 19 18 17 16 15

To my great teacher, Thay Thich Nhat Hanh,
and to all of my monastic family–
thank you from the bottom of my heart.

Contents

Introduction

I'd like to begin by stating for the record that I never planned to write a book. It just sort of happened. Well, that's not true entirely. Being an inherently lazy person, if I had known just how much blood, sweat, and tears go into each page of a book, then I don't think I would ever have begun. This book began as a series of talks, one each week, that I gave during the annual winter retreat of 2012–2013 at Deer Park Monastery in California, which were offered as a structured learning course for friends at home who wished to follow along with the three-month retreat. While being very dedicated practitioners, many friends lead very busy lives, and wish for a way to bring the winter retreat's spirit of focused learning and practice into their lives, since it would be well-nigh impossible for them to step away from their responsibilities for three months.

Each week of our retreat started with a forty-five

minute talk on a particular theme, and included readings, suggested practices, and questions that practitioners at home could reflect on, alone or together with a Sangha or group of practitioners for discussion. In fact, many Sanghas throughout the United States and around the world followed along, listened to the podcast, and used the reflection questions as topics for group discussions.

It was my intention to create an atmosphere of intimacy and informality through having these sharing sessions: I wanted participants to feel as though we were chatting together as good spiritual friends. The great teacher Shantideva is reported to have said, "Everything I want to say has already been said, and I am destitute and poor of expression." A truer thing has never been said with regard to me and to my teaching. Many wonderful meditation manuals, sutra commentaries, and technical books on Buddhism exist, but this small volume does not pretend to be any of those things. It is not as much of a "how to" as it is an invitation to "just do."

I intend this book to be like a kind spiritual friend who will take your hand and walk with you on your path, wherever you find yourself in this moment. I invite you to take a chapter each week and read it slowly over the course of a few days, allowing the words to sink into your being. In the same way as on a formal retreat, I've provided suggested readings, practices, and questions for reflection in each chapter. You will find it helpful to have a notebook handy to write down your insights and reflections as we move through these next weeks together.

Each year, the Buddhist monastic community holds a three-month retreat in which we focus all of our time and energy into our spiritual life. It is a time when we also concretely experience the beauty of the Sangha jewel, the gift of community, one of the Three Jewels of Buddhist practice. The Rains Retreat, as it is called, is a central practice of Buddhist monastic communities in all traditions— Theravada, Mahayana, and Vajrayana. It's so central that when we ask each other how long we've been ordained, we don't reply, "Ten years" or "Five years" or "One year," we say, "I've completed *x* number of Rains Retreats."

Traditionally, since the time of the Buddha, the Rains Retreat has been held in Asia in the summer months when the monsoons bring heavy rain, and it's very difficult to travel around; naturally, our focus turns somewhat more inward. Especially in Europe, and also in North America, where I'm currently sitting, the summertime is a really easy and wonderful time to travel around. Individuals and families find it easy to come to the monastery, and we go out to offer retreats and Days of Mindfulness throughout the country. The wintertime is when it's rainy or snowy and it's cold and difficult to travel around. Therefore, in the Plum Village tradition, we hold our annual Rains Retreat in the winter, usually beginning in mid-November and ending in mid-February.

There's a great need for structured learning and practice. Through this humble book, I offer an opportunity to those of us who don't live near a practice center to encounter the depth, the simplicity, and the beauty of focused practice. Each of the ten chapters is a heart-reflection on some of the core teachings of Buddhism and contains suggested practices. I suggest you dedicate some time on your calendar toward your own self-retreat. While it's not necessary to stick to a strict schedule, I suggest that you move through this book slowly, one chapter a week, either for your own personal practice or with a group of friends, in person or online.

As we practice over the next ten weeks, let us be aware that we're not practicing in isolation, even though it might seem so at this moment if you are sitting by yourself. An important part of our annual Rains Retreat is the opening ceremony, when we declare the physical boundaries of the space that we will be practicing in, and when we take refuge in each other for the duration of the retreat.

In a monastic setting, during the Rains Retreat we don't set foot outside the physical limits of our community. The outer physical boundaries that we choose to remain within help us to focus on what's really necessary and most important. They help us to develop focused attention, to release our scatteredness, and to let go of a lot of our busyness. It's so easy to get carried away with any number of different things that we think are crucially important to do now, and, despite the best of intentions, we get carried away from what we most wish to do, which is to live our lives deeply and meaningfully. But the outward boundaries don't mean much if our minds are still running around here, there, and everywhere. The presence of outer boundaries facilitates an inner process of letting go and the deepening of a sustained personal practice.

At the very beginning of this journey, the very beginning of our time together, consider your own situation—wherever you might be, and whatever you might be doing, what your focus of attention might be as you work through the reflections and exercises in this book. What is the clutter that is filling up your space—both outer space and inner space?

What are the outer boundaries that we might find helpful to declare for ourselves? For example:

- "During these next few weeks I'm not going to spend four hours a day watching TV."
- "In October and November I'm going to take a walk every lunchtime and practice walking meditation every day."

- "From New Year's Day until the first day of spring I'm going to commit to meditate every day."

What are some of the inner boundaries you might find helpful to declare for yourself? Some examples might be:

- "I recognize that I get caught up in self-judgments and judgments of others. During this period of practice, when I notice that habit energy arising, I will breathe deeply, smile, and let go."

- "I notice that I am often worried or anxious. During these weeks, I will consciously practice to bring myself back to the wonderful present."

I would advise you not to try to be too ambitious—two or three intentions are probably more than sufficient for most of us.

Balance Your Spiritual Life

Not so long ago, my teacher Thich Nhat Hanh, whom we call Thay (teacher) according to Vietnamese tradition, gave a very beautiful teaching to the monastic residents of our community, in which he shared the importance of creating a dynamic balance in our spiritual life. He talked about our spiritual life as being composed of four aspects: study, practice, work, and play. When we live in a balanced way, these four areas form a harmonious pattern or mandala of practice in our daily lives.

1. Study

The first area of our spiritual life is study. During the annual Rains Retreat at Plum Village, Thay almost always focuses his teachings on a particular text. Cultivating a mind geared toward learning is a beautiful aspect of monastic life. The very first element of the Eightfold Path, the path outlined by the Buddha that leads to liberation, is Right Understanding. There is always something more to discover, some way to grow.

Throughout our lives we will encounter wonderful and profound teachings. Each time we encounter a teaching, we need to ask ourselves, "How does this relate to my own practice? How can I apply this in my own life? Does this teaching have anything to say to me right now?"

I often share with my friends that it's essential to recognize that almost all of the sutras begin with the phrase "Thus have I heard." When we read a sutra, when we hear a teaching, it's not only a teaching being given 2,600 years ago, it is being given to us right here and right now. It is the living Dharma—the gift of teaching that leads to understanding—and is the second of the Three Jewels of Buddhism. What are you hearing when you encounter a text or a teaching? What's the teaching that is speaking to you in this moment? What is the living Dharma that's touching your heart right now? I've got to tell you, I don't know how many times I've gone through all of the sutras in my chanting book, since every day we have at least one chanting session. Perhaps I've recited each sutra a few hundred times—that's a very conservative guess. And yet honestly, every time I hear those sutras, something new leaps out at me. It's almost as if through day-to-day practice the ground has been prepared so that I hear a teaching in a way that I haven't heard it before. It's not the same every single time. It's easy to think, "Oh, I've heard that sutra or teaching before," and to stop listening. To my mind, that's a shame.

When I was in Oregon offering some teachings a few years back, I was offered a beautiful calligraphy by a calligrapher at the retreat. It's very simple; it says: "Each Moment Only Once." Each time we encounter a sutra, a teaching, a person, an experience, are we able to approach it with fresh eyes, letting go of our preconceived notions? This is a very subtle practice.

2. Practice

The second of the four areas of the mandala is practice. In my Buddhist tradition, of course we have sitting meditation, but we also have walking meditation, eating meditation, listening-to-the-bell meditation, and stopping meditation! Everything has the breath as its foundation: each type of meditation is an opportunity for us to return again and again to our breathing.

We don't want our spirituality to be something that we do in our spare time, or a chore that we have to make time for. Rather, in our practice of what we call "Engaged Buddhism," it is our very lives that are our practice, the expressions of our deepest aspiration. This means every moment, however mundane, has the potential to be a moment of enlightenment. The person in the car in front of me as I'm sitting in my car at the stoplight; my coworker who is having problems at home; the bell that's on my right-hand side; that person in the Sangha who always rubs me the wrong way: they are all opportunities to develop our heart. In fact, Thay always reminds us that our meditation practice should be a joy and a delight.

We can make the choice to approach each moment as a moment of practice. I hope you don't get the idea that it's always easy for monks and nuns. It's not really. You may think that in life outside the monastery there are always too many distractions and things that need to be done, which are constantly drawing attention away from "your spiritual life." To walk on the spiritual path requires a real commitment. Please don't think, "Ah, it's so easy for the monastics. They don't need to worry about anything—they have an easy life, sitting on the mountain and watching the butterflies." Come up for a couple of weeks and see for yourself! You'll find that even in the monastery there are plenty of distractions and mountains of work; however we do our best in each moment to approach each activity as our spiritual practice.

Making the commitment to yourself to embark on this journey is challenging, since you are making a choice that goes against so much of your conditioning. It is, however, one of the most rewarding choices you will ever make. Please make your commitments very simple. It might be, "Every day I'm going to enjoy one meal in mindfulness," or "Every time the phone rings I'm going to enjoy three in-breaths and out-breaths before I pick up," or "I'm going to be present with my Sangha every week even though that person is going to be there too," or perhaps, "I'm going to enjoy a period of sitting meditation every day." Please don't try to be too ambitious; in fact it's good to keep it *really* easy. We might be tempted to make commitments like, "I'm going to wake up in the morning and do 108 prostrations and then have an hour of sitting meditation and chant three sutras and the Three Refuges and then the closing verses and end my day with another period of...." We've all struggled with this tendency at some time or other.

Please don't try to re-create the schedule of a monastery or practice center at home. Start where you are, in the situation you find yourself in right now, by making a few simple choices to enrich your life. I would suggest keeping it really simple, so that we can maintain our commitments and experience the joy and fulfillment of keeping them! I've noticed that the things we judge as "unimportant" are often good indicators of our avoidance strategies. We tend to try to cover over things by making big showy commitments. Yet it's the very simple things that will transform our lives. In the Plum Village tradition, the way we live creates continual reminders that our meditation practice should be a joy and a delight.

Concretely speaking, in addition to choosing some simple practices such as stopping and breathing every now and then, taking some steps in walking meditation each day, and enjoying a mindful meal, I recommend that you set aside a few minutes at the beginning and the end of the day to simply sit. Five or ten minutes might seem like an impossible task at the beginning, but by making this commitment to your self, you are bringing the best possible energy into each day. Don't underestimate the transformative power of five minutes of simply sitting.

3. Work

The third area of spiritual life is the element of work or service. If we feel isolated, or depressed, or alone, often a way to begin the process of transformation is by reaching out and being of service where we are right now. For some of us, our path of service is a paid position in a company: we have a job working in a company, or we run a business. Some of us take care of our families; others of us are unable to work, but concentrate our efforts on recovery or healing. Can we see all these as paths of service? One concept that we will be exploring together in some depth in later chapters is that of the *bodhisattva*. In simple terms, a bodhisattva is a being who has vowed to be of service to others. Can we be bodhisattvas wherever life has planted us? I don't want to say too much about the element of work at this point, because it's my observation that here in the United States we're very hard workers already. If truth be told, we might be a little bit too skillful in this aspect!

4. Play

The fourth area of the spiritual life that Thay invites us to look into is the element of play—choosing things that we find delightful to do, which really nourish us and water the seed of joy in our lives.

Our practice is not hard labor—it's not something for

which we grit our teeth and sweat big bullets of perspiration, and then finally break through to the other side. This is not meditation practice in the Plum Village tradition. Thay has always shared with us that one of the distinguishing features of the Dharma at Plum Village is learning how to arrive at our destination in every moment.

The practice of play is really a practice of being at ease. I love the word *ease*, don't you? Just saying it out loud is relaxing thanks to the beautiful open vowel sounds. I dare you to say it slowly out loud, especially if you are in a public place. In 2000, I traveled to the United Kingdom with Thay and a delegation of monks and nuns. One morning, Thay suggested that we visit the British Museum to look at the mummies. In order to get there, we needed to take the London Underground subway network, which everyone calls the Tube. At that time of the morning, there were still many people traveling to work and so we monastics needed to stand in the aisle. As the train began to move, Thay turned to us and said, "Everyone looks so sad, let's cheer them up." He asked us to sing, "Happiness is here and now, I have dropped my worries, nowhere to go, nothing to do, no longer in a hurry," for the commuters. I was mortified. (This was a long time before the phenomenon of flash mobs.) As the singing started, I tried to edge my way away from the group of monks and nuns, and I stared stoically out of the train windows. I was sure that people were waiting for us to whip the hat around for a donation or two. Halfway through the song, Thay noticed I wasn't singing and called out, "Sing louder, Brother Phap Hai!" I began to lip-synch, but couldn't bring myself to sing out loud. When the song ended, there was a brief pause and I could see the commuters looking at us, waiting to see what would happen next. What happened next was that we monastics just smiled and turned to look out of the windows. At that moment, laughter broke out in the carriage and the passengers passed around a smile. When we arrived at the next station, as people were exiting the train many of them expressed their thanks.

So don't be too shy to be playful—you might just make someone's day. The day you make might be your own!

One of the wonderful ways that playfulness can manifest is through a practice of laziness. At Plum Village, Lazy Day is a day for us to be truly present to the day without any scheduled activities. We just let the day unfold naturally, timelessly. It is a day in which we can practice however we like. For some of us, to have a weekly Lazy Day can be almost impossible. But we can always find time for one hour a week of laziness. *There is time.* We fill up our days with so many different things. I invite you to—at least once a week—find time for laziness. For me, laziness means to do that which delights me most in terms of the practice.

One time Thay was asked by a member of our community to rename our Lazy Day, which is a Monday, to Personal Practice Day, and Thay said: "No, I'm not going to rename it 'Personal Practice Day.' I'm going to keep it as 'Lazy Day.'"

Laziness is one of the hardest things for people in our modern society all over the world to practice. We think we're being "lazy," but we spend all our time watching TV and reading books and writing emails and catching up on errands and paying that bill and seeing this or that person. Laziness, in the Plum Village practice, means to allow the world to be as it is and to allow each moment to unfold just as it unfolds: to experience the beauty, as I am right now, of the morning sun coming up; to watch the sky changing; to see the wind blowing in the leaves.

How incredibly healing this is! How important it is for us. I often joke with my friends that I think we could change the culture here in North America and other busy places by the simple act of initiating a national daily nap time, as people do in a number of countries in southern Asia and southern Europe. Just give everybody, say, forty-five minutes after lunch: an hour's lunch break and then forty-five minutes when everybody just practices total relaxation. Let's imagine that for a minute. We're so driven in our daily lives to work, to achieve, to accomplish, and we can often bring this same energy to our spiritual lives as well. We are not projects; we're not things that need to be fixed. We need to bring the elements of ease, relaxation, and joy into our lives of spiritual practice.

So how are you manifesting the energy of playfulness in your practice? I find as I travel around visiting different sanghas that many meditation practitioners are too serious; they've lost a lot of their lightness and humor. I think we can be very serious practitioners *and* be very, very light and joyful. I actually think it's essential to play if we're going to go far on the path. I know that I can't take myself very seriously when I see the stories I tell myself. How about you? A few weeks ago, a friend came to visit our monastery for the first time and at the end of her stay she shared that she was impressed by the solid energy, and yet she was surprised because she had expected the monks and nuns to be much more solemn. It was a revelation to her to see that in addition to "formal" periods of practice our spiritual life is expressed through joyful interaction, sports, and the echo of laughter amongst the mountains.

Stay Open and Receptive

There are three attitudes to look out for that can be very challenging for us in our life of practice. They are likened to three pots. The first pot is a full pot; it's a mind that's full of opinions and ideas: opinions about ourselves, opinions about others, ideas of right and wrong—in short, many ideas. Our mind can be very, very full, so full that it is difficult to receive a drop of the Dharma. Buddhism is not about gaining a whole lot of intellectual knowledge, but rather about transforming our hearts and waking up to our real situations.

There's a second kind of pot, which is described as a pot with poison in it. The image that's given is that of a person whose mind is very critical, cynical, or judgmental toward other people, members of our Sangha, the way things *should* be, and often—and sometimes even more harshly—toward themselves.

The third pot has a hole in it. We can imagine a pot full of water, and yet some is pouring out of the side because there's a hole in it. This image relates to someone with a very distracted mind, who's always daydreaming. The energy built up by spiritual practice cannot develop or ripen, because it's not being held.

As you go through the next ten weeks or so, be aware of your attitudes toward the teachings, and try to be receptive and open.

The Story of Sopaka

The framework of this book is based on a very simple and beautiful text from the Pali canon that I love deeply. It is called the Samanera Pañha from the Khuddakapatha, and it consists of ten questions that the Buddha asked a young novice called Sopaka, which basically cover all of the core Buddhist teachings to become an *arahant*, a person who is far advanced on the path of Awakening. The commentary on the Samanera Pañha tells us that there was once a boy called Sopaka, who was seven years old. When he was very young, his father had passed away, and his mother had remarried to a gentleman who didn't like him at all—in fact, he hated him. Perhaps he was jealous of his wife's love toward Sopaka, or maybe he found it annoying to have a child around—there could have been any number of reasons—and he treated him very badly. In our day and age, we would say he abused him.

At a certain point he got so tired of Sopaka that he said to the boy, "Oh, why don't you and I go for a walk; we haven't gone for a walk for a long time. Let's go, you and I, and we'll get to know each other." So Sopaka, the poor little seven-year-old boy, went walking with him. The stepfather took him to a charnel ground, a place like a cemetery where corpses are burned and left to the elements, and he chained the boy up to either a gravestone or a corpse, depending on which source you rely on. I believe that it would have been a corpse, since it took place in India and they didn't commonly have graves then; typically bodies were burned.

In chaining him up, the stepfather had the intention that Sopaka would be eaten by the wild jackals who scavenged the charnel grounds. He hated him that much.

It was getting dark, and poor Sopaka was terrified when his stepfather left him there. As it was getting dark a shape appeared, and it was the Buddha, who happened to be walking by. He saw Sopaka and asked the tearful boy what had happened to him. Sopaka shared his story, and the Buddha untied him and brought him back to the Jeta Grove Monastery. The Buddha bathed him, gave him food to eat and clothes to wear, and he consoled and comforted him.

I love that image of the Buddha. When I read this story, I wonder why it hasn't received more attention in the many commentaries on Buddhist teachings. It's a beautiful image of the loving kindness that the Buddha manifested toward this traumatized boy. I'm sure it must have taken many months, if not years, to console and comfort this poor little boy.

The story continues that when the wicked stepfather—those are exactly the words with which the stepfather is described in the commentaries—returned home, Sopaka's mother asked, "Where is my son?" The stepfather replied, "I don't know where he is; he must have come home before me; he ran away." But the mother was frantically worried about her son, and she couldn't sleep at all. The next day she went to see the Buddha and asked him what to do. The Buddha saw her from a distance and asked, "Why are you crying, sister?"

"I only have one son and since last night he's run away. He's been missing. My husband took him for a walk and the little boy never returned home. He never came back."

The Buddha said, "Don't worry, your son is safe. He's here. He's taken refuge with us." He brought Sopaka out, and Sopaka was reunited with his mother.

Sopaka asked the Buddha for permission to become a monk, and his mother agreed, so he was able to become a novice monk and practice in the community with the Buddha. He was very young, and in the traditional texts they called young novices like that "crow-scarers"; they ran around scaring crows away. So I imagine from time to time he was a little bit naughty, but I also see how much care and love the Sangha must have offered him.

The story doesn't end there. Sopaka later became an arahant, a great practitioner, and realized the Way. When he was getting toward the age when he was ripe for full ordination, the Buddha summoned him and asked him a series of ten questions, and Sopaka was able to answer all of the questions. The Buddha, on the basis of Sopaka answering those questions from his own experience, allowed him to receive full ordination.

What is said to be one?

All beings subsist on food.

What is said to be two?

Mind and body.

What is said to be three?

The three feelings.

What is said to be four?

The four noble truths.

What is said to be five?

The five constituent groups of mind and body.

What is said to be six?

The six internal sense spheres.

What is said to be seven?

The seven factors of Awakening.

What is said to be eight?

The noble path with eight factors.

What is said to be nine?

The nine abodes of beings.

What is said to be ten?

When endowed with ten factors he is said to be Worthy. [*]

It's very early in the morning today, and I'm sitting in the Moon Over the Mountain Peak meditation hall in

---

[*] Khuddakkapatha 4, Translated by Bhikkhu Anandajoti. https://suttacentral. net/en/kp4. The original translation was released under the following license: Creative Commons Attribution-ShareAlike 3.0 Unported License.

Deer Park Monastery near Escondido, California. The sun is just beginning to shine through the windows; it's such a beautiful morning. I'm visualizing all of you, all the different places you're sitting right now and reading these words, and I'm wishing you all well.

These ten questions form the framework that I have chosen for this book. The title of each chapter is based on one of the questions asked by the Buddha. Each chapter presents an opportunity for us to experience the vastness of the Buddha's teachings; each teaching is like a gate or Dharma door through which I'm inviting you to walk. They're very simple questions; they have very simple answers. And yet they're very profound. There are chapters in which I discuss the answers Sopaka gives in the text, and in some chapters I have brought in other answers to the questions, elements that I've found are helpful on the path. For the most part, each chapter builds on the one before. In later chapters, we will often touch on material that was presented earlier in a new way.

Are you ready to embark on your journey?

CHAPTER ONE

The One Thing That Nourishes Us All

Practicing One Hundred Percent

The other day I sat down and calculated I've been a monk for eighteen years now. During that time, I've been asked *a lot* of questions. I'm okay with that, since Buddhism is a spiritual path that is based on asking questions—questions of our teachers, questions of each other, and, perhaps most importantly, questions of ourselves. The vast majority of the sutras in the Buddhist canon came about thanks to someone asking the Buddha a question. We monastics also get asked many questions, and there is one question that we get asked most often. I wonder if you can guess what it might be?

At least once or twice a week, a friend will come up to me and ask, "Brother Phap Hai, I'd like to ask you a question. Why did you become a monk?"

The question is a good one, and yet recently I have found that it is less important to relate why I became a monk eighteen years ago, and more important to respond with how I experience my spiritual life today and why I continue to be a monk. My relationship to my life of practice is like any relationship—it grows, it changes, and it deepens over time. Questions are important. Some of the most important questions we must ask ourselves (and each other) are:

Why am I a meditation practitioner?
What brought me to the practice?
What is it that I'm seeking?
Why am I still practicing?
What does my practice look like in this moment?

Reflecting on these questions both individually and collectively helps us to identify our motivation and provide a direction for our practice. Let us ask ourselves the third question listed above: "What is it that I'm seeking?" Write down the first answer that comes to you. There's no wrong answer, really—unless of course it's something like, "I'm an outgoing Sagittarius seeking a well-balanced Gemini for a mutual vision quest."

When we sincerely ask ourselves this question, any number of answers may arise, for instance, "peace," "happiness," "enlightenment," and so on.

Look at the word that you wrote down a moment ago,

perhaps "peace." Now, let's go a little bit deeper. What does the word "peace" mean to you? What is the experience of "peace" for you? What are some of the moments of your life in which you have experienced "peace"? What did it feel like in your body?

I find it interesting that often when we're considering a deeply personal and intimate part of our lives, such as our spirituality, we use very general words elucidating grand concepts such as "peace," "happiness," "liberation," and so on without taking the next step of exploring what such words or concepts mean to us—or if they mean the same thing to others. Although there are some commonalities, one person's happiness is not necessarily another person's happiness.

I was reminded of this in 2010 when my younger brother Benjamin and his wife came to visit me in Deer Park Monastery. Our parents had both passed away when we were quite young, and we had not had a lot of opportunities to get to know each other as adults. When Benjamin came to Deer Park, I asked him what he would most enjoy doing together. He told me that he wanted to go to Universal Studios with me and have fun on the roller coasters. I brought up his request to the other monks in our next meeting, secretly hoping that they would say no. The brothers all said, "Brother Phap Hai, you should definitely go." So off we went to Universal Studios. It had been perhaps fifteen years since the last time I'd been to an amusement park. So much had changed in that time. I didn't know, for example, that at the end of each ride they snap pictures for souvenirs. Consequently, in every picture taken of us on the rides, you can see everyone else's hands in the air and broad smiles on their faces and then there's me—with my eyes screwed shut and face pale as a ghost.

What is peaceful or liberating for one person may be oppressive to another. Since we all have different sufferings, strengths, weaknesses, and tendencies to work with, one person's practice will not look the same as another person's practice. As you allow yourself to sink down to a deeper level within the big words—the big concepts—and touch the soft, tender core of your being, you will discover your motivation, or what is called in Buddhist psychology "volition"—the energy that moves you forward. What is it that *you* are looking for?

In 2012, Thay gave all of the monks and nuns a little white card that had "100%" written on it. It was a lovely reminder from him that the essence, the core, of the Plum Village practice is to be present, to be undivided, one hundred percent of the time. What a challenge this is for us in our modern society where we put such a value on multitasking, of not "wasting" a single second. Consciously choosing to do one thing at a time has become the ultimate countercultural and revolutionary act.

Children know how to mono-task, how to absorb themselves completely in whatever they are engaged in at the time. We have lost much of this wonder and become jaded.

In one sense, developing meditative concentration is about relearning how to mono-task. Whether we're walking, sitting, standing, or whether we're together with others, we are fully present, body and mind. We have arrived.

In Plum Village centers all over the world, the word that we hear most often is "arriving." In 2000, I was invited to travel to Australia to help offer retreats and Days of Mindfulness in various cities. Our delegation flew from Bordeaux to Paris, and then from Paris to Dubai. From Dubai we flew to Ho Chi Minh City and then to Sydney. By the time we landed in Sydney, we had been traveling for over forty hours. I will never forget walking up the stairs to my room: the suitcases I was carrying seemed so heavy. Stepping into my room, I placed them down and a big "aaahhh" rose from the core of my being: a moment of relaxation, a moment of bliss. Until that moment, I hadn't realized how tight and tense my body had become during the long journey. My whole body relaxed; I felt my breath flowing in and out. I felt wonderful. I had arrived at my destination.

The practice of arriving is a practice of allowing that "aaahhh" to manifest in each moment—each breath, each step. To be fully here. This one practice alone is worth a lifetime of practice. I call it "ahhh-riving."

Suggested Practice
Ahhh-riving

What are the "bags" that you might be carrying within you right now? Perhaps you have a to-do list that is as long as your arm, worries, anxiety, discomfort in your body.... As you breathe in, connect with your body, your breath, this moment; and on your out-breath allow an "aaahhh" to flow through your whole body and mind, and let go of all tension. You might find it helpful to vocalize the "aaahhh." Don't be afraid to have some fun with this. For this week, if you notice yourself becoming tense or disconnected during your day, return to this practice of "aaahhh." At the end of the week, I suggest that you take some time to evaluate the impact of this practice.

As practitioners, we practice arriving with the sensations in our bodies, with our in-breath and out-breath, and with the thoughts in our minds. When we cultivate the capacity to be fully present, we are cultivating an energy that we call mindfulness (*sati*). Mindfulness is a natural quality of our mind. Cultivating mindfulness can enrich our lives since this simple, bare awareness helps us to rediscover the wonder of our everyday human experience. Walking, breathing, eating—all of these commonplace actions that we usually give no thought to—become deeply wonderful.

Many of us have grown up with the idea that there is a fundamental separation between body and mind, the so-called Cartesian split. We see consciousness as centered only in the brain. Through this concept we can mistake spiritual practice as only an intellectual exercise, rather than an embodiment.

I would like you to try an exercise right now: close your eyes, breathe in and out, and then using your right hand, point to yourself. Where is your finger pointing? Were you pointing at your head or your heart? When I have done this simple exercise with groups, approximately ninety percent of participants point to their heart—the core of their being. Our bodies are great teachers, and when we can allow ourselves to arrive in our bodies, we discover much wisdom contained therein.

In the Vedic philosophy common to the Buddha's time, the seat of consciousness was seen to be the heart and, by extension, the whole body. How does it change our approach to cultivating "mindfulness" if we change our focus from our brain to our heart, or to our whole body?

Sati can also be translated as "re-collection" or "re-membering." I like these translations very much. To re-member or re-collect is to bring all of the disparate parts of ourselves back to the here and the now.

In the Plum Village tradition, our fundamental practice is the development of mindfulness of breathing. In its simplest form, this means to notice that you are breathing in, and then breathing out.

Suggested Practice

Quietly Observe the Breath

Find a quiet place, where you can sit or lie undisturbed for a few minutes. Bring your consciousness back to your body and simply notice your breath as it flows in and flows out. If you find it helpful, as you breathe in, you can note: "in"; as you breathe out: "out." Remain resting with your breath for a few minutes. It can be wonderful to begin and end our day with this practice.

Whether we're sitting, or walking, or eating, we bring a gentle and loving awareness to our breath. Cultivating mindfulness is a gift that we offer ourselves and not a fight or a struggle.

As we develop an intimacy with our breath, with our body, and with the world around us as it unfolds, we begin to notice the places and the situations in which we hold back, when we're not as open as we could be. We start to discover our patterns of closing down, of running away. I like to call these "the places we hide" or sometimes "the tracks in the carpet."

I used to love visiting my grandparents' house. Until the late 1980s, it was still decorated in prime 1970s style: brown and orange wallpaper, avocado-colored cabinets, and mustard-colored chairs. One of the things I loved most was to lie down on their shag pile carpet. Over the years, pathways or tracks began to appear in the carpet: a track to and from the kitchen, to and from a particular chair, and so on. My grandparents had definite pathways that they used to walk.

We too have our "tracks in the carpet"—neural pathways that we continually travel down, habit energies that continually manifest, our daily rituals. In order to cultivate an authentic transformation of the heart, we need to understand that meditation is not a place to hide or to "get comfortable," but rather to engage with life, as it presents itself to us in each moment. As we develop the capacity to be present with our experience, we begin to notice our habitual patterns, and we're able to smile to them.

Even though intellectually we can grasp that the essence of the practice of mindfulness is to choose to be present in every moment one hundred percent, most often we struggle against where we are, what we're doing, or who we're with in this moment due to the "tracks in the carpet" we've created for ourselves. We want to be somewhere else, with someone else, doing something—anything—else.

Mindfulness is always mindfulness *of* something. It is grounded and established. We can bring mindful attention to our breath, to our body, to our feelings, to our thoughts, to contemplate a situation, and so on.

When I was a very young practitioner in the early 1990s, I had the opportunity to take a basic Buddhism course in a Chinese temple outside of Brisbane. During one of the lessons, the reverend asked us what we thought meditation was. We went around the circle for the participants to offer their responses and when it was my turn, I answered, "Meditation is about balancing the microcosm of the body with the macrocosm of the universe." The reverend, to her eternal credit, looked at me with a lot of compassion in that moment and simply shook her head before we moved on to the next person. When everyone had answered, the reverend looked at us and shared that Buddhist meditation was learning to bring our mind to rest on one point.

I love this description of meditation. As we develop our capacity to be present with our bare experience (mindfulness or sati), naturally it deepens into concentration (*samadhi*). Concentration in Buddhist meditation is not the kind of concentration that we usually associate with studying for exams and that leaves us exhausted after a few hours. It is described as "bringing the mind to rest." Have you ever walked far on a hot, sunny day and then sat down under a large, shady tree, with your back resting against the trunk? This is the experience of concentration in Buddhist meditation. I have also heard concentration described as plunging into a cool lake: most refreshing!

I'm reminded of a teaching Thay gave to us back in 1998. He shared that in the Plum Village style of practice, one hour of study should equal seven hours of practice; for every hour of book learning, we need to have seven hours of putting it into practice, of actually applying it. Many of us are very good at learning a lot of Buddhist terminology and concepts: reading Dharma books, sutras, commentaries, and so forth, but we're not so good at actually taking these practices and applying them to our daily lives. Have you ever wondered why that is? How might it relate to the "tracks in the carpet," our habit energies or comfort zones that we mentioned earlier?

Searching for Happiness

When we look at our situation, we see that at some level we—together with all beings—want happiness, peace, and joy; we want to solve our difficulties. This is natural; this is human nature. This is also the root of the Buddha's discovery and it's a great thing! However, if we're really honest with ourselves, we have to admit that we keep looking in the wrong places. We keep looking for the wrong things. We place our reliance on things that just provide a temporary fix, something or someone outside of ourselves that we think is going to heal that wound we have within. We're always looking for the thing that we think is going to fix us. We think that we need one more condition, just one more thing.

If we hold this attitude, however subtly, we begin our practice life not by deeply trusting in our own innate goodness and the innate goodness of others, but rather we see ourselves as "broken," as needing to be "fixed." We approach the practice with an attitude of lack, rather than an attitude of abundance. We're looking for something, someone, a condition that we think is outside of ourselves and that is going to "fix us," to make it better. With this mindset, the focus of our spiritual life becomes all about fixing ourselves. We think that we're bad, and so we create ourselves into a fixer-upper project. I myself have noticed that whenever I've made myself into a project, along with becoming quite harsh and judgmental toward myself, I become quite harsh and judgmental toward others, and then other people turn into my fixer-upper projects.

In the Discourse on the Eight Realizations of the Great Beings, a sutra our teacher loves very much that is included in the Plum Village chanting book, *Chanting from the Heart*—there's a really powerful phrase. It reads, *Our mind is always searching outside of itself and never feels fulfilled.* It's always running after the next thing. This is where the Buddha's teaching is really radical, because the Buddha basically tells us, "You do not need even one more thing; you are already what you want to become."

Among the many stories told about the Buddha's awakening, there is one that I feel is important for us to understand deeply before going any further: that one of the first things the Buddha is reported to have said when he awoke was, "Whoa, this is strange; not only me, but every living being has the seed of infinite goodness, of infinite kindness, of awakening, within themselves. Every living being will become a Buddha." We call this capacity the seed of *bodhicitta*—the mind of love.

To put this in another way: the approach of Buddhist practice is to uncover the innate wholeness that has always been there—the natural state of your mind. As Thay says,

"We are already what we want to become."

As I write these lines, we are in the end-of-year holiday period. In the United States, this begins with Thanksgiving in late November and extends through the winter holidays. This season is a great time of year to reflect on our relationship to abundance. One of the important teachings for our time is the three-word mantra, "I have enough," or, "We have enough." Many of us, especially in the developed world, enjoy such material abundance in our lives. Thanksgiving is an opportunity for us to really look and see the conditions of happiness that we already have. Many of us do this quite well on Thanksgiving Day itself; we celebrate the blessings that we have. The intriguing thing for me is that the day after Thanksgiving, after we've celebrated all of the wonderful conditions that we already have, we start looking for something else. Black Friday, as the day after Thanksgiving is called, is the biggest day of the year in terms of sales, when people run out to buy this, to buy that, because we think we need one more thing, or we want to get one more thing for somebody else, especially at a bargain price. I find this very interesting, this urge to run after things the day after we've spent a day in gratitude for what we already have!

Here in Deer Park we also celebrate Thanksgiving in our own way. We have a Dharma talk on the Four

Gratitudes; a gratitude walking meditation during which we reflect on the many kindnesses we've received over the past year; as well as a ceremony expressing our gratitude to our blood, our spiritual, and our land ancestors, and to each other; and then we have a potluck Thanksgiving lunch. On the day before Thanksgiving, we normally go around to all of the businesses and all of our neighbors—in a very wide geographical area—and we offer them homemade egg rolls—it's like reverse trick-or-treating.

A number of years ago, Thay called me into his hut and said, "Rather than running around looking for small comforts that take the edge off your dissatisfaction, your discomfort, you need to discover the Great Comfort." These little things that we go running after—fame, position, other people's approval, a free upgrade from coach to first class (which has never happened to me, by the way)—are described in the Buddhist commentaries as "licking honey off the edge of a razor": it's temporarily very sweet, but if you lick too much honey, you're going to experience something else entirely when you get to the razor's edge. Many of us are at that razor's edge, aren't we?

Instead, try to recognize deeply once and for all the truth in the mantra, "I have enough": you have so many wondrous and healing conditions in your life and heart and you—yes, *you*—have the capacity to transform your suffering, awaken, and be a resource for others on the path. All of these conditions are available to you in this very moment and you have no need of even one extra condition. There is great power in this recognition. "But"—I hear you saying, "What about my_____ (insert your problem or condition)?" You have enough. What is preventing you in this moment from letting that light and beauty shine forth?

Suggested Practice
List Your Supportive Conditions

What are some of the supportive conditions you experience? They might be external, such as a job you enjoy, a good relationship, good health, time for spiritual practice, and so on, or they might be internal, such as the capacity to forgive, a sharp mind, motivation. List them down and celebrate them, even if they seem insignificant. Save your list of supportive conditions in a safe place and return to it often, especially in difficult moments. You may find that you add to the list over time.

The Four Nutriments

The very first question the Buddha asked the young novice Sopaka in the text is, "What is the one?" Sopaka reflected for a moment, and the answer recorded in the text is that he said, "All things subsist on food," meaning, the one thing that connects everything is that all things exist on nutriment.

In the Buddha's teaching, there are four aspects to nutriment. It is perhaps most clearly described in the Buddha's Discourse on the Four Kinds of Nutriment. It's a very profound contemplation on the four different kinds of nourishment for the body and mind.

1. The First Nutriment: Edible Food

The first kind of nutriment is edible food, which means what we put in our mouths. It can be argued that the things we put in our mouth may not necessarily be edible food in this day and age! But for the sake of our discussion here, the things that we eat are considered edible foods.

When I first encountered the Discourse on the Four Kinds of Nutriments, I admit that I was taken aback by the bold imagery the Buddha used in his teaching. I think the Buddha offered such very strong examples because he wanted to underline the importance of nutriment in our daily life. He wanted to shock us a little. The Buddha tells us the story of a couple going through the desert. They've run out of food; they've run out of water. They're carrying their son on their backs. They realize that there's absolutely no way for them to cross the desert if they have nothing to eat, nothing to drink. So, in this heartbreaking story, we discover that the couple decides that the only way they're going to survive is through killing and eating the flesh of their only child.

The Buddha asks the question, "Do you think that they ate that flesh with a lot of rejoicing and happiness, a lot of joy?" and everybody says, "Well, of course not." The Buddha invites us to look at all edible foods in the same way. How do the choices I make affect others?

Let us ask ourselves the questions, "Through choosing this particular kind of food, what resources am I taking? What resources am I using?" This brings us to the realization, "If I consume massive amounts of resources, or eat in such a way that it damages my own body, then this is like eating my son or daughter's flesh."

One Native American tradition has the famous invitation: "Let us reflect on the effects of our decisions for seven generations in the future." We can ask, "What kind of effects does this choice have on the world around me and on the future?" We use a lot of resources in our daily lives—especially through our choices around edible foods. How far has this food traveled to get to me? Do I really know where it comes from? How much water is in the food? How much grain is in the food? Is this actually food at all? All of these questions can be extremely helpful reflections for us.

Ask yourself, "How is this food nourishing my body?" "How is it nourishing my mind?" "How is this food healing me?" These kinds of reflection develop a helpful and healing relationship to the food we put in our mouths. This nutriment is the most straightforward of the four nutriments for us to practice with since it has to do with our physical bodies.

In the Plum Village tradition, we emphasize the practice of mindful eating: being aware of the food, looking deeply into the source of the food, looking deeply into all the different conditions that have come together to create this food that we're now bringing into our bodies. Do we stop and become aware of all the different conditions that have come together to create the meal that we're eating? For example, we're invited to look into a carrot and connect with the sunshine, the rain, the farmer who grew it—all the different conditions that have come together so that the carrot can appear on your plate. Are we really aware of the taste of the food? Do we chew our food thoroughly? You know, sometimes people think eating meditation is a very superficial and simple practice. But in the Plum Village tradition it's important to bear in mind that while we eat just to eat, while we walk just to walk, while we sit just to sit, all of these practices have elements that carry over into the rest of our lives.

When we practice eating meditation deeply, we can discover many things. Let's take a very simple example. Let us imagine that we have a spoonful of food, and we've placed it in our mouth, and we're chewing the food. While we're chewing the food we notice that we're preparing another spoonful; many of us do this. We already have a mouthful of nutriment, we're already nourishing ourselves, and yet we're preparing another one! What does this say about the way that we interact with the food we consume in our daily lives? This is a question we can ask ourselves. The Plum Village practice really helps us, through its simplicity and its depth, to discover the habitual ways that we do things.

Suggested Practice
Eating Meditation

Each day this week, choose one meal when you will allow yourself time and space to enjoy the process of nourishing your body and mind. You may only be able to find ten minutes, but those ten minutes are very precious. Turn off the TV, silence your mobile devices, and allow your eating to be a meditation. Sit comfortably and notice how you are feeling in your body: How does hunger feel? Do any emotions come up? Notice the food that is in front of you: its color, its fragrance. Why did you choose these particular foods? Take a bite and chew the food slowly, at least thirty times, paying attention to its taste, its texture, and your inner reactions. Consider the sources of the food. Notice when you have an urge to swallow and take another bite. As you progress through your meal, notice how you are feeling in your body, and notice the moment when you feel that you are satisfied. Often, if you are tuned into your physical sensations, you will feel satisfied before you have finished eating all of the food on your plate.

We're so sure we know what it is to eat, what it is to walk; we think we already know what it is to sit, and yet one of the first things we will discover as we begin to practice is that we do so many of these things unconsciously. When we approach these overlooked and almost forgotten moments of our lives with some awareness, we begin to relearn and rediscover what it is to eat, what it is to walk, what it is to sit, and we become more and more alive. Each moment becomes a moment when we have an opportunity to encounter the Dharma. These activities of our daily lives are not lost or wasted moments. They are life itself—they are our practice itself. They can be a moment of opening our heart, of waking up, if we choose to allow them to be so. It's really up to us; it's up to us to choose to be there, to choose to allow this moment to be a moment of awakening or a meaningless moment. No one else can do that work for us.

Marcel Proust reminds us, "The real voyage of discovery consists not in seeking new landscapes, but in having new eyes." In our time it's a luxury to be able to sit down and have ten or fifteen minutes for mindful eating. Perhaps we don't have that block of time available in our day, but we can make choices such as to turn off our phones, the TV, the radio, and so on for a few minutes so that we can be fully present for the nourishment we're offering ourselves. This is an act of self-love and an act of love for our society.

2. The Second Nutriment: Sense Impressions

The second kind of nutriment is sense impressions: the things we see, hear, smell, taste, and touch. In our daily lives, we don't notice the majority of the sense impressions that come to us. We're bombarded daily with an incredible amount of input through our senses! If you are experiencing a great deal of mental fatigue, bring your awareness to your sense impressions—the sights and sounds that we come into contact with every day. The sheer volume of impressions we receive each and every day just through advertising is overwhelming.

Sense impressions live on within us, as Marcel Proust so famously recounts in his novel *À la recherche du temps perdu*, known in English as *Remembrance of Things Past*. One day, the narrator sits down with a cup of linden tea and a *madeleine*, which is a small French cake. He dips the madeleine into his tea and upon taking a bite, the taste and smell open up a path of involuntary memories for him, and he finds himself transported to earlier experiences and times.

I am no Proust, but to this day, whenever I smell fruitcake, I'm transported back to my grandmother's house. She was a cake decorator and her house always smelled very strongly of fruitcake, which we call plum pudding in Australia. I have such a strong connection with that smell.

An evocative scent carries many of us back to different experiences we've had during our lives. This is also the case with a taste, a sound, a sight, or even a sensation in our body. These are also forms of nutriment. Many of us come home in the evening feeling utterly exhausted and overwhelmed. It might have something to do with the number of sense impressions we've had during that day, things that we haven't been aware of. The image for sense impressions that the Buddha gives in the Discourse on the Four Kinds of Nutriment is the image of a cow with no skin being attacked by insects. It's very apt, isn't it? Sometimes we feel like a cow with no skin. Yet rather than returning home to our breath, to our body, to our mind, we continue to allow ourselves to constantly be pulled in all directions.

Suggested Practice

Beginning to Notice
Sense Impressions

One good way to begin working with sense impressions is to start by noticing sensations that arise and pass away in your body as you are doing sitting meditation. After sitting for a few minutes, invite your mindful attention to rest in your body. Notice how your body feels—tense, relaxed, warm, cold. Notice the sensation of your body touching the chair or cushion, and the spaces between your body and the cushion. Notice where your clothes are in contact with your body. Gradually, as you settle into this experience, notice any tingling, itching, prickling that might be occurring. Notice sensations as they arise and what subtle emotions manifest in you as a result of them.

Once you have established this practice, notice where your eyes are drawn and the things you look at; notice everything that feeds your senses in turn—the sounds, the smells, the tastes—and your reactions to them.

3. The Third Nutriment: Volition

The third kind of nutriment is described using the term "volition." We might also describe it as "that energy which moves us forward." Sometimes we use the words "aspiration" or "intention." In our life of practice it is essential both to identify and to set our intentions. An intention is very different from a goal. A goal is something that we hope to attain in the future. An intention, on the other hand, is something that we set our heart upon and begin to manifest right here and now.

As we move through our life of practice we become increasingly aware of the subtle intentions that we bring to each encounter, to each moment. What is pushing me forward? What is moving me forward in this moment? Is it a wish to connect with others, a compassionate intention, an intention of love? Or is it an intention of closing down, of getting something for me?

We have to be very careful what we wish for! In 2005 during Thay's return to Vietnam, we had the opportunity to go on silent almsround in Hue. An almsround is a traditional practice in many Asian Buddhist communities, in which the monastic members either stand or walk silently with a begging bowl for food. By that time we had been traveling around Vietnam for about six weeks and, while I love Vietnamese food, I was really craving a piece of bread, which was less common to find there. As we walked slowly through crowds of people on the almsround, I received rice, steamed sweets in banana leaves, salted tofu, and various fruits. We monastics are only permitted to receive food offerings up to the rim of the begging bowl, which is traditionally known as the Vessel of Appropriate Measure. At the halfway point of our walk, my bowl was almost full. Suddenly a woman placed a piece of fresh baguette and a wedge of Laughing Cow cheese in my bowl. I felt as if all of my Christmases had come at once and I kept walking on, delighted. As I continued on my way, more offerings were placed in my bowl until it threatened to overflow. When a Vessel of Appropriate Measure is full, if we receive an additional offering, it is customary to offer something back to the giver in its place. It almost tore my heart out, but I had to offer back the precious baguette and cheese in order to receive an offering of rice from an older lady.

We sat down under the cool shade of the trees to enjoy our lunch silently, and while my lunch was delicious, I couldn't stop thinking about the baguette and cheese. Afterward we stood up to make our way back in procession to the Root Temple. On the way out of the park, an elderly gentleman holding a pink plastic bag made a beeline straight for me. He thrust the pink bag into my hand and disappeared back into the crowd. Upon returning to the Root Temple, I peered inside the bag and discovered four fresh baguettes and a box of Laughing Cow cheese!

In the first verse of one of the earliest Buddhist texts, the Dhammapada, the Buddha is quoted as saying: "Mind is the forerunner of all things; they are ruled by the mind and depend on the mind." I've noticed that life often seems to present us with what we expect to receive. In other words, our intention or motivation contributes to creating our reality since that drive is the lens through which we view the world around us.

The image the Buddha offers for "volition" in the Discourse on the Four Kinds of Nutriment is that of glowing embers. This quality of love is an essential quality of the path. Without this warm heart, our practice is, or will soon become, dry and boring.

In the Mahayana tradition, one very important practice is to develop our mind of love. Thay has written a whole book on this called *Cultivating the Mind of Love.* The "mind of love" is another way of translating the Sanskrit term bodhicitta, that which moves us forward to awakening and helps us to reach out of our small comforts into connecting with others and being present for others. I think Pema Chödrön describes it very well: "our soft spot," that place where we're ourselves, we're less guarded, and we're able to meet others and the world around us openly.

4. The Fourth Nutriment: Consciousness

The fourth kind of nutriment is consciousness itself, or more specifically, the seeds in our consciousness. The Vijñanavada school of Buddhist psychology describes fifty-one of these seeds: seeds of happiness, seeds of joy, seeds of peace, of understanding, of mindfulness, as well as seeds of anger, jealousy, hatred. These are also forms of nutriment. The image that the Buddha gives in the sutra is that of a criminal repeatedly pierced day and night by three hundred spears.

Understanding how nourishment works is one of the most important things to know in our life of practice. Everything exists on nutriment; our happiness didn't come from nowhere, and our peace didn't come from nowhere; in the same way, our anger didn't fall from the sky. As we develop our mindful awareness, we become increasingly aware of the choices that we make with regard to the things we come into contact with, and recognize the sources of nutriment that nourish our joy, our peace, our happiness, our bodhicitta, and the sources of nutriment that nourish our anger, our sadness, our isolation. Discovering the sources of nutriment within and around us in every moment begins to empower us to make wise choices. Thay calls this "selective watering," watering the beneficial seeds and choosing not to provide nutriment to the things that at this moment in time bring suffering to ourselves and to those around us.

Selective watering is a challenging practice because most of the time, just like the honey on the edge of a razor blade, the things that bring us suffering can seem very sweet indeed.

As a practitioner, at a certain point we realize in our

bones that we've played this story out so many times, over and over and over again. This is the meaning of samsara, which is a Buddhist term meaning "the endless round." When I was in New York, I saw a cartoon that sums this up perfectly. The caption read, "Samsara: the same damn thing over and over again." We're like the insane person in Einstein's definition of insanity—doing the same thing over and over and expecting a different result. When we finally realize our insanity, it is usually a stimulus to try different approaches. We start to experiment, because we're tired of playing out the same old story: licking the honey off the razor blade over and over again. At that point, a beautiful quality manifests in our lives: renunciation, or letting go. This is a natural turning away from things that are not in line with our deepest aspiration—there is no struggle here at all.

People often think that monastic life must be so tough, so hard, because we have to "give up" all of the fun things of life. I am a cheeky person so when someone says that to me, I like to ask them to tell me what fun things they are thinking of. I've gotten all kinds of responses over the years—everything from "all-inclusive cruises" to "bacon." The truth of the matter is that at a certain point in our life, certain things like cruises and bacon just don't interest us anymore. Rather than closing ourselves down from life, renunciation becomes about opening up to the many possibilities that life presents to us—not getting caught in a limited view of who or what we can become.

When I was in elementary school, I was in love with coleslaw. I wanted it for lunch every day. I would beg my mother to let me have coleslaw for lunch. She gave it to me for a while, but as we moved into summer, one morning she told me that I couldn't have it because the mayonnaise would go bad in the heat. I begged and pleaded and even cried a little bit, and she finally gave in. I had my coleslaw each day for lunch, and God it was good! But one day, sure enough, the mayonnaise went bad, and after I swallowed it, the coleslaw made a very rapid reappearance.

I was so sick! From that day forward it became difficult for me to enjoy coleslaw at all. At one point in my life, I think it would be fair to say that coleslaw got me out of bed in the morning, but after what I like to call "The Incident," I have never been able to feel the same way again about what was once my favorite kind of food.

We all have our version of coleslaw, if we're honest. At a certain point we're just so glutted on a certain behavior or a certain idea that it becomes the most natural thing in the world to let it go and expand our horizons. Each one of us has things we hide behind and each one of us can benefit from stepping out from our hiding places and entrusting ourselves to our hearts and to the universe. There is a great joy and freedom in this.

The Four Noble Truths and the Nutriments

The Buddha invites us into the practice of reflecting on the Four Noble Truths as they relate to the nutriments. If we visualize the Buddha's teaching as a wheel, The Four Noble Truths form the central point of the wheel from which all the teachings and practices spring. They are not just concepts or beautiful ideas, but practices to transform our lives. They're practices for us to apply in our daily life in every situation we encounter.

The First Noble Truth is recognition: "I'm recognizing what is taking place." "This is my real situation." Then moving to the Second Noble Truth, we look deeply into the root of that situation: it might be my happiness, or it might be my anger. Through looking into the root and source of that situation, a realization manifests that there is a way out. This is the Third Noble Truth. We discover the ways that we've nourished this situation, the ways that we've contributed to the arising of this situation, and we discover a way out, the Fourth Noble Truth. This is the practice of Buddhism: to apply the Four Noble Truths to our daily lives and to generate understanding and compassion.

As we look at the four kinds of nutriments, questions arise: "How do I nourish myself?" "What are the ways that I make good choices to nurture and care for myself?" "How do I nourish my beloved ones, my Sangha?" And, "What are the ways that I don't nourish myself, or that I pretend to nourish myself?" "What are the ways that I don't nourish my beloved ones and I don't nourish my Sangha?" "What are the ways that I shut down or close up?" "When I look at my own unique situation and the difficulties that I encounter, what are some of the ways that I've nurtured that suffering?"

Meditation as Daily Nourishment

One of the most important teachings in the life of a practitioner is the cultivation of joy. I think this is such important medicine for us. We can tend to get very serious about our practice or about the spiritual life; it becomes something solemn and rigid.

We are reminded of the importance of taking in the joy of our practice as daily nourishment. If we don't enjoy and take delight in our practice, then we're not going to go very far. What do you need to do in order to enjoy your practice? I am in full agreement with the wonderful writer Anne Lamott when she shares, "Laughter is carbonated holiness."

When we look at ourselves, we usually tend to focus on our negative qualities. If we hold this attitude toward ourselves—and we do, let's face it—then for sure we will tend to manifest the same attitude toward others. We beat ourselves, and others, up a lot.

Never forget that at the very core of the Buddha's teaching is the truth of our basic goodness and the basic goodness of all beings. I think for many of us it's easier to focus on the good qualities of other people (well, sometimes at least!) than it is to focus on our own positive qualities and our own basic goodness. One form of nutriment that I share about from time to time, since I often see that we forget to apply it in our daily lives, is the practice of rejoicing in the wholesome deeds and the wholesome qualities of ourselves and others.

Suggested Practice
Reflecting at the End of the Day

It can be a powerful practice to spend time each day focusing on the situations in which we've opened our hearts and recognized beautiful qualities in ourselves and in others. It's so wonderful to reflect on our basic goodness! Most of us tend to reflect primarily on the times that we've held back, the areas that we've shut down, and while this is useful and essential for our growth, it needs to be counterbalanced with the conscious recognition and celebration of our positive qualities. That which we pay attention to grows stronger.

For the coming week, at the end of every day take time—perhaps five minutes—to go through the whole day and reflect on those moments and situations when the basic goodness in yourself and in others has been apparent. Through this practice—which is actually delightful and runs counter to our cultural conditioning—we nurture our bodhicitta, our mind of love. We also begin to develop *mudita*, empathetic joy, which is the mind of love toward others. We rejoice in the good deeds and qualities that arise in ourselves, and those we see arising in others. It's a very beautiful practice.

It is also a lovely practice to reflect on the awesome and wonderful qualities in each of the members of your family and in each of the members of your Sangha. How often do you take time to nurture and express your gratitude for the wonderful qualities that we see in each other? This can be powerfully transformative. What are you waiting for?

CHAPTER TWO

Two Truths

Applying the Practice in Our Daily Lives

Each of the teachings that we're exploring together is a concrete tool for us to apply in our daily lives, a lens through which we can contemplate and understand our own unique situation more deeply. They're not just concepts for us to think about.

When we initially encounter one of the teachings, we may receive it primarily on the intellectual level and that's great. That's a very good beginning. In fact, we should take a few breaths to celebrate the fact that we have the opportunity to encounter transformational teachings and to understand and apply them at whatever level we are able. The Buddha, when asked to describe how rare it is to encounter teachings and practices of liberation, gave this simile:

"Imagine that there is a vast ocean with a wooden plank floating around on the surface. There is a small hole in the wooden plank. Deep in the ocean is an ancient blind turtle who surfaces once every hundred years or so for air. It is more likely that upon surfacing for air that the head of the blind turtle will emerge through the hole in that wooden plank floating randomly on the surface of the great ocean than it is for someone to encounter transformational teachings, have enough capacity to understand them, and to put them into practice."* We have planted very good seeds indeed!

There are many deep, marvelous, and, indeed, mystical teachings of the Buddha. Whenever we encounter a teaching, we need to always ask ourselves: How can I apply this teaching to my own situation? Is this a useful teaching for me at this time? Each of the teachings and practices that we are exploring together are different frames through which we can view our situation, and some are going to be appropriate for us right now, some maybe later, and some maybe not at all.

I'd like to get something important out of the way right now: Not every teaching and practice will be useful and suitable for you. Each one of us has different capabilities,

---

* Chiggala Sutta. Samyutta Nikaya 56.48

different tendencies, and we all encounter the teachings differently depending on these and other factors, such as life experience and early environment. I'm often reminded of this when I'm in retreat. Usually after hearing a Dharma talk, we sit together for a Dharma discussion about the topics that were raised. If there are thirty people in the discussion group, each person may have been struck by a completely different aspect of the talk. It's almost as if we've heard thirty different talks! I myself find that each time I listen to one of Thay's talks, I hear something I haven't heard before.

When an individual decides to enter the monastic life, he or she enters a period of preparation for full ordination and takes novice vows or precepts. In the recitation of the precepts for novices, there is a line that reminds us not to "waste our time and our youth." In recent years as I've traveled around and practiced with so many friends from many different backgrounds I've begun to see this teaching in a new light. I have started to believe that the biggest waste of our time is comparing our practice to that of others. Our authentic spiritual lives begin when we give ourselves permission to embrace the particular journeys that we need to make. Each of us has our own unique struggles and strengths.

We receive the teachings that we are ready to receive. This is one of the most wonderful and exciting things about the Dharma for me. Whenever I feel that I have understood a person, a practice, a situation, or a teaching fully, a new layer reveals itself. We are always growing and changing from moment to moment. In the same way, we need to cultivate an attitude of allowing our practice to grow, to change, and to evolve over time; otherwise our practice becomes simply a set of techniques rather than a pathway of understanding. We can get stuck on the form, the technique, rather than the transformational experience that the technique engenders.

A number of years ago, Thay shared with the community that if we're doing the same thing in twenty years, then we have failed. When I heard this, I was reminded of the time after my father died when my mother needed some extra money and rented out a room to a young man. Every morning he would wake up and have two bowls of shredded wheat, a slice of toast, and a cup of orange juice for breakfast. Day in and day out he would have the same thing for the year and a half that he stayed with us. I joked with my mother at the time that I wouldn't get out of bed in the morning if I knew exactly what was coming for breakfast each day.

Life has a funny way of keeping us honest, doesn't it? Now I live in a monastery. In the world it is said that there are two things we can't escape no matter how hard we try—death and taxes. In the monastic life, there are also two things that we can't escape no matter how hard we try, and yes, I have tried—early morning meditation and oatmeal for breakfast! Evidently Thay wasn't referring to monastic breakfasts when he encouraged us not to keep doing the same thing for twenty years.

Our monastic schedule is very regular year-round. When I was visiting family last year, they asked me how I can stand to do the same thing day in and day out, week after week, year after year. I thought for a moment and responded that if I allow myself to be fully present, then each day, each moment is never the same. The sameness of our everyday routine actually frees us up to transform ourselves afresh each day.

Even though I practice mindful breathing and mindful walking every single day, each time I practice, I experience my step and my breath in a new way. We call this newness and freshness "beginner's mind." If you notice yourself finding your practice dry or boring, consider whether you might be thinking that you've got it all figured out already.

Each time I read about the history of Buddhism, I am reminded that we are incredibly lucky people: earlier generations did not have the access to the teachings that we have today. Perhaps they only had the chance to encounter one sutra, or one book on Buddhism, or hear a talk from a teacher once, and that was it. Maybe they traveled many days or weeks to ask a question like, "What is the essence of the Buddha's teaching?" and the teacher replied, "Look at the cypress tree out front!"—as ninth-century Zen Master Zhaozhou responded to a monk who questioned him about the teachings—and sent them on their way. Nowadays there is a wealth of Dharma materials available at the click of a button. We are indeed fortunate. At the same time, this period is often called the "Dharma-Ending Age." Why, in the midst of such an outflowing of Dharma material, could this possibly be called the Dharma-Ending Age? Seems kind of counterintuitive, doesn't it? As I was contemplating this, I felt that the great challenge, the great distraction of our time is the accumulation of piles upon piles of information and, simultaneously, our lacking the capacity or the motivation to put much of it into sincere practice. This is a great pity, and yet it is the situation that we find ourselves in today.

In early November 1998 I traveled with Thay to the German-speaking countries of Europe to offer retreats, Days of Mindfulness, and talks. I treasured that time together with Thay. One afternoon in Zurich we were sitting and having tea together. Thay pointed out of the window at a large oak tree whose branches were almost bare in the cold wind, except for one branch that still had a few autumn leaves remaining. Thay commented, "If the tree wants to grow larger in the spring, it needs to let go."

If we want to make room for growth, we need to be willing to let go of practices that no longer serve us— practices which, rather than liberating us, have become dry, stale techniques or ideas that we hide behind.

The Buddha offered a vast number of different teachings and practices over the four decades of his teaching ministry. There are the Four Establishments of Mindfulness; there's the Noble Eightfold Path; there are the Four Noble Truths; the teaching of Dependent Origination; the Two Truths; the Paramitas; and so on. Each of these teachings are invitations, different frameworks for us to use to look deeply into our human situation and to transform our hearts. Perhaps a certain framework will be useful and suitable for us at a particular time in our practice life, and then, as we grow, transform, and evolve, a different container is necessary. If I'm thirsty, a cup is necessary to hold the water to relieve my thirst, but if I focus all of my attention only on the cup and never drink the water, how will I resolve my situation?

Don't get too caught up in the framework itself. The framework is a skillful means of presenting ultimate truth— and ultimate truth cannot be fully expressed through concepts, ideas, and language. How on earth will we ever master all of the teachings? By deeply entering one of them.

Taking the example of nutriment that we discussed

in the previous chapter, we can begin to use nutriment as a framework for contemplation in daily life by bringing awareness to edible food. This is the simplest—edible food is right in front of us where it's easy to see; it's very concrete. Sense impressions and volition are more subtle, and awareness of these will be easier after we develop our capacity to be aware of edible foods. Once our attention can easily rest with edible food and we're able to contemplate it deeply, we can bring our attention to our sense impressions and consider the nutriment we receive from these. Perhaps we begin noticing the things we see, the things we hear, but we mustn't forget to ask ourselves the question: How are these things nutriments, and what exactly are they nourishing?

It's the same thing with our motivations; we used the term "volition" previously. *That which moves us forward—* how is that a nutriment and what is it nourishing? This becomes a grounding for our practice and continues to deepen and deepen until insight develops.

The same is true for the arising of consciousness and awareness itself. This is also a form of nutriment. In Buddhist Psychology, when we speak of "mind" in the simplest terms we are speaking of "Mind Consciousness" our everyday aware mind—and "store consciousness," which is roughly equivalent to the subconscious mind. In the Vijñanavada (Mind Only) school of Buddhism, store consciousness is described as consisting of fifty-one seeds (*bija*) which can be further categorized into wholesome seeds, not-yet wholesome seeds, and indeterminate seeds. Some examples of these seeds are happiness, delight, mindfulness, and anger. They exist in "seed" form in store consciousness until they encounter a stimulus, at which time they rise into our mind consciousness as a "mental formation." A major fruit of Buddhist meditation is a process of becoming increasingly familiar with our own inner landscape and learning how to cultivate beneficial seeds that will bloom into beneficial mind states. This is the fourth form of nutriment: consciousness.

The Guidebook and the Journey

Each of the Buddha's teachings is useless unless it is applied. A useful analogy might be studying a guidebook before we embark on a journey. We can gain an incredible amount of knowledge about the sights, landmarks, and places to stay from the guidebook. However, it all remains theoretical until we put the book down and actually embark on the journey, using the information we learned to help us on our way. To be a real traveler we need to set down the guidebook and begin *our* journey, wherever we may be right now—to breathe the air of our new surroundings, to taste the local delicacies, and to enjoy serendipity.

As much as we would wish it to be different, we cannot make anyone else's journey. We need to make our own. A guidebook is essentially somebody else's journey, a record of someone else's discoveries. The Buddhist teachings are like a guidebook to the greatest journey we can imagine. They are the discoveries of the wise ones, the great teachers who have made this journey before us. They point out the landmarks for us to use in embarking on our own journey—wherever we are.

In 2010, I was invited to help facilitate a Day of Mindfulness at the beautiful Ojai Foundation in southern California. We arrived late in the evening and immediately went to sleep in our cozy yurt. The next morning, I woke up early and noticed that next to my bed was a little pamphlet that contained a map of a "gratitude walk" meandering through the beautiful grounds. Realizing that this would be a wonderful way to start the day, I pulled on my coat and picked up the map. Stepping out of the front door, I looked around to get my bearings and then glanced down at the map. Drawn on the map was an arrow and three words: "You are here." I started walking in the pink dawn and after a number of minutes walking, I didn't seem to be in the place indicated on the map. Nonplussed, I turned and retraced my steps back to the yurt and then started walking in the other direction. There was the same mismatch between where the map indicated I should be and where I actually was. At that moment in time, I have to say that I wasn't exactly experiencing gratitude! I realized that I had been caught up in the arrow and the three words, "you are here." While it is certainly true that "I am here," I was not in the "here" indicated on the map.

I breathed in and out and realized that I had all the information I needed. I put down the map. Taking slow and gentle steps, I began walking and after a while I arrived at a place called the deep kiva. From there I made my way to the teaching tree, under whose wide green embrace Thay gave Dharma talks back in the 1980s. Over the course of the next hour I explored the grounds, trusting my step and the journey that I needed to make, beginning from where I needed to begin.

A guidebook or a map is important for us to know what landmarks are out there and as a tool to use on our way. But the decision we actually need to make is to put one foot in front of the other and embark on the journey, to take it from the intellectual level down into the level of experience. The Buddha's teachings, like a map, give us an outline of the journey, inner and outer, yet each of us will enter the path at the point that's appropriate for us; and, if we let go of our idea of how things "should" be, then we are free to begin walking the path that is our own unique expression of the Dharma.

In Plum Village centers worldwide, we have a verse that we call the Sutra Opening Verse, which we recite before reading any of the Buddha's teachings: *The Dharma is deep and lovely. We now have a chance to see, study, and practice it. We vow to realize its true meaning.* What does it mean to you to see the Dharma? Are you able to see the Dharma right in this moment? What Dharma is present for you?

In 2004 during the Rains Retreat at Deer Park, I was spending some time with Thay and he turned to me and said, "Brother Phap Hai, in Mahayana Buddhism there is a teaching that there is nothing that is not Dharma, nothing that is not a teaching if we are fully aware."

Whenever I recite the sutra opening verse, I look back at myself and often I'm forced to concede that I'm pretty good at hearing and studying the Dharma, but not so skillful at "seeing" the Dharma in my daily life or putting the Dharma into "practice."

The true teaching is not contained in words. The familiar old Zen saying reminds us that the spoken and written teachings are like "a finger pointing to the moon"; it points the way and shouldn't be mistaken for the moon itself. Teachings are being transmitted in each moment—through the sound of the wind in the trees, the warm sunlight, our mindful breath and bodily interactions—if we allow ourselves to be available for them.

The importance of our physical presence and bringing awareness to where we find ourselves in our daily lives was brought home to me a number of years ago soon after I had first arrived in Deer Park. Traveling the world, I have always found it interesting to visit local supermarkets and see which foods are popular. So my trusty sidekick Brother Phap Dung and I went down to the local Vons supermarket in town, and after wandering around we eventually found ourselves in the snack aisles marveling at all of the different varieties and flavors of chips and snacks that were on offer. As we were standing there, in something akin to awe, a woman approached us. She took one look at us then grabbed a large bag of chips off the shelf. As she continued down the aisle, she remarked, "I knew I was on the right path!"

Practicing with Intelligence

The Buddha was a sensitive and profound teacher. Often he gave different answers to the same question, depending on the capacities and tendencies of the questioner or the audience. The Dharma is often described as medicine. We should apply those practices that immediately speak to us and that are really helpful at this point in our journey, and not wrestle or struggle too much with those that don't resonate at this moment in time. If I don't have a stomachache, then there's no reason for me to take an antacid. Taking the appropriate medicine for our situation is called practicing with intelligence.

All of the monks and nuns in Plum Village centers share the cooking, the cleaning, and other chores. During my novice years in Plum Village, I had the opportunity to be on the same cooking team as a young female meditation practitioner from Taiwan. One morning, I saw her taking some Chinese herbal medicine and I asked her if I could have a taste. "Sure," she replied, "it will make you strong." Being someone who loves the taste of Chinese medicine, I took a big mouthful and thanked her. It was only then that I asked her the question that I probably should have asked in the beginning: "So, what's it good for?"

"Women's problems," she replied.

A word for the wise: Don't be like me and take medicine for complaints that you don't have—even if that medicine is Dharma medicine. If we are able to bring mindful awareness to our situation, we can diagnose some of our spiritual "complaints" and find the appropriate practices to help us transform them.

We all have our blind spots. One of the great gifts of living in community is that the community can often see us more clearly than we see ourselves. It can be a powerful practice to ask our community to share with us the spiritual complaints they see we could use some Dharma medicine for. In our monastic community we practice this formally at least once a year and we call it the practice of Shining Light. Our Sangha, our community of practice, is a great teacher, a great embodiment of the wisdom of the Buddha.

If you find that some teaching or practice does not resonate with you right now, it's okay; don't suffer too much. It may not be the time for that particular practice or, just as in the story above, you may not need that particular kind of medicine. If we take even one of the practices and we apply it fully and sincerely, we can go very far. We can allow those teachings and practices that don't really fit for us right now to rest in the fertile ground of what we call our store consciousness or latent memory, and allow them to sprout and grow if and when it is time for them to do so.

Mind and Body

In the second week of the Rains Retreat we asked ourselves the second question that the Buddha posed to Sopaka: What is two?

The traditional answer to the question that is recorded in the text is "name and form," mind and body—or in Pali, *namarupa*, which we'll be exploring in depth in chapter five.

Wisdom and Compassion

In the Mahayana tradition to which I belong, there's another "two" that is essential: wisdom and compassion. Wisdom and compassion have to go together like the two wings of a bird. Wisdom or insight—*prajña* in the Sanskrit language— is not intellectual knowledge. Intellectual understanding forms a good foundation. But it's only that—a foundation. Insight here is exactly as it sounds in English; prajña means seeing something from within—to *inner*-stand something. I think that's really important for us to grasp. We are not separate from the object of our attention.

The practice of asking ourselves, "Am I sure?" is a wonderful invitation for us to move beyond our limited idea or the "conventional designation" of something. For example, we look at a banana and right away we call it a banana because we believe that we know what a banana is and we don't go beyond that superficial level. We look at a phone, and we call it a phone—that's what it is, and that's all it is. This is okay on one level—we need to use these common terms of reference to live our daily lives, but the problem here is that we do the same with our happiness, our enlightenment, our delusion, *samsara*, *nirvana*, a buddha, or a sentient being. We label things so quickly in daily life. We think we know what a buddha is, we think we know what a sentient being is, we think we know what a banana is. And with this limited view these things seem to be very separate from us indeed.

In the Plum Village tradition, we speak a lot about "interbeing," the interdependent nature of all that is. Thay teaches us to be able to see the cloud in a sheet of paper, to be able to see all generations of ancestors in every cell of our bodies. So then, why do you think that the Buddha and sentient beings are separate? Why do you think that happiness is a separate thing, entirely removed from suffering? We create a world of duality, of subject and object, of this and that, of me and you; of in-breath being entirely different and separate from out-breath.

In 1999 we had the chance to visit the great Zen Master Linji temple in the north of China. As we walked in, I happened to glance at a section of calligraphy that read "Not Two" or "Nonduality."

This is because *that* is.

Labeling is normal and natural; it's what we must do in our everyday life in order to function effectively. We need to understand that there is a deeper level beyond the concept called "the label." Our teacher Thay's invitation into this awareness is for us to ask ourselves, "Am I sure?" whenever we notice ourselves labeling. Am I really sure that I understand what the Buddha is? Am I sure I understand what my happiness is, that I understand who you are, that I understand who I am? If we're really honest, I think we have to answer no. We can't be too sure. And yet I don't think we're that honest with ourselves in daily life; if anything, we err on the side of being too sure. We're too sure of how things should be in ourselves, in others, in our Sangha, and certain we know what the right way is to do things.

The other wing of the bird is compassion. Compassion is described in the texts as a quivering of the heart, such as when we look at the situation of others and three words arise in our consciousness: *"just like me."* Compassion is the concrete manifestation of wisdom; it is wisdom applied. If we just have wisdom and no compassion, it's a very cold, dry wisdom. If we only have compassion and no wisdom, we end up getting completely burned out and we don't really know the right way to be able to help anybody, including ourselves.

True wisdom and compassion manifest on the ground of understanding our interconnectedness. In a retreat held at Saint Michael's College in Vermont in 1998, Thay taught that the invitation of the Diamond Sutra is for us to generate the understanding that there is no distinction between the gift, the giver, and the receiver. Thay told the story of a time that he hit his thumb with a hammer. Without one hand blaming the other or thinking, "I'm helping you," without any thought at all, the uninjured hand grabbed the hurt thumb and held it, trying to take away the pain. It's a natural reaction. There's no idea that I am giving something to you, but it's the absolutely natural response in that situation.

The Dalai Lama also puts it very beautifully: "Regard all living beings like they're our mother." In Plum Village we encourage the development of what we call "a spirit of generosity infusing our practice." How is our practice an offering to ourselves, to our loved ones, and to those around us? What is our aim? Is it something small like my own peace, my own joy, my own liberation? Or is it something larger? A small aim can be a good place to start, but it's only a start. Over time we're going to progress. How does the spirit of generosity and non-separateness, the spirit of giving and receiving infuse my own practice?

Offering the Dharma

I think for many of us, it's much, much easier to give than to receive. We find it quite difficult to receive gifts from others, whether it's a compliment, a gift of money, a gift of a book, or the gift of somebody's presence. In receiving we're also giving; in giving we're also receiving.

In the Buddhist texts, there are three kinds of gift that are described. There's the gift of material things: books, money, clothes, a meal, and so on; there's the gift of nonfear—that's a very lovely gift to offer, the gift of solidity, of fearlessness;

and then there's the gift of the Dharma. As monastics, who don't have that many material resources, we do have the opportunity to offer the Dharma. In terms of possessions, we've got three robes and a bowl; if I pull your name in our annual Secret Santa, prepare yourself to receive a nice rock or a pinecone rather than an iPad! But the offering of the Dharma is described as the supreme gift, the gift that surpasses all the others, because we're offering methods, tools for people to be able to transform their suffering and experience true joy.

Questions for Reflection

What would it mean to you to offer nonfear? To yourself? To others?

What does it mean to you to offer the Dharma, and how is that different from offering advice?

The Ultimate Dimension of Reality

Another of the tools that may be useful for us to consider are two pairs, each of which we can call the Two Truths. They are the historical dimension versus the ultimate dimension, and conventional truth versus absolute truth. The historical dimension is our everyday reality of pairs of opposites: of mornings and evenings, of beginnings and endings, of this and that, of left and right, of me and you, of up and down. This is indeed one level of truth; however, there is also another aspect to reality that we call the Ultimate Dimension, which cannot be described in words and notions—any concept will fail to adequately describe the ultimate nature of reality.

Suggested Practice
Labeling

As you move through your day, notice the many times that you label and categorize objects, experiences, and people: telephone, banana, morning, evening, happiness, brother, sister, pleasant, unpleasant, boring, and so forth. When you notice yourself labeling, take a few seconds to see if you are able to connect with another layer of reality.

Everything depends on our way of perceiving. After the Buddha was enlightened he was walking on almsround in a small village. He encountered a local cowherd who was surprised by the Buddha's radiant and peaceful expression and who asked him, "Are you a god?" The Buddha replied, "I'm a fully enlightened one." The cowherd shrugged his shoulders, saying "Maybe, friend, maybe," and continued on his way.

In a deep, secret place in our hearts, most of us are

supremely confident that if the Buddha walked past us right now, we would recognize him or her. Here we have a cowherd who came face to face with the Buddha and shrugged his shoulders and walked on.

Do we understand fully what it is we are seeking, whether it be happiness, liberation, or peace? Perhaps the quality we are seeking is not that far away after all, not something that we need to work hard for seventy-five years to find, but that has been right under our noses all along. Are we really able to touch liberation, joy, peace—whatever word we want to put there—right now? And if not, why not?

Our story is a little like the story of the destitute beggar in the Lotus Sutra who's been running around in abject poverty without knowing that all along he's had a priceless jewel sewn into his jacket. Master Linji, the great Zen master I mentioned earlier, tells us to stop all of our running around after external conditions, come back to ourselves, and discover everything that we're looking for right here, right now, in the present moment.

Suggested Practice

Gratitude

That which we pay attention to grows stronger. Take a few minutes throughout your day to bring your awareness to "conditions of happiness" that present themselves to you. They might be very simple things indeed—good eyesight, warm clothes, or a nice cup of tea.

Do you enjoy your practice? One day when I was still a young novice, I was sitting on the edge of the wooden deck of Thay's hut with my legs hanging over the side. Thay was lying behind me in his hammock, and together we were looking over the grapevines in the distance. After a few minutes, Thay said, "Brother Phap Hai, if you're going to sit there, make sure that you swing your legs."

Of course, Thay was not only talking about me sitting on the deck, but he was offering me a teaching about my way of relating to my meditation practice. In my early years of practice, I tended toward being too stiff, too formal, and in that process, there was not much enjoyment and delight.

What do you enjoy most about your meditation practice? Enjoyment isn't something that we reflect on a lot, is it? What is it that's life-giving for you about your practice?

Reading

from The Diamond That Cuts Through Illusion

Opening Gatha

How may we overcome the fear of birth and death

and arrive at the state that is as indestructible as a diamond?

What way can direct us in our practice

to sweep away our thousands of illusions?

If the awakened mind shows its compassion

and opens up for us the treasure store,

then we may bring into our lives

the wonderful diamond teachings.[*]

Reading

from The Diamond That Cuts Through Illusion

Selections from the Discourse

This is what I heard one time when the Buddha was staying in the monastery in Anathapindika's park in the Jeta Grove near Shravasti with a community of 1,250 *bhikshus*, fully ordained monks.

That day, when it was time to make the almsround, the Buddha put on his *sanghati* robe and, holding his bowl, went into the city of Shravasti to beg for food, going from house to house. When the almsround was completed, he returned to the monastery to eat the midday meal. Then he put away his sanghati robe and his bowl, washed his feet, arranged his

---

[*] Thich Nhat Hanh and the Monks and Nuns of Plum Village, *Chanting from the Heart: Buddhist Ceremonies and Daily Practice* (Berkeley, CA: Parallax Press, 2007, 2013).

cushion, and sat down.

At that time, the Venerable Subhuti stood up, bared his right shoulder, put his knee on the ground, and, folding his palms respectfully, said to the Buddha, "World-Honored One, it is rare to find someone like you. You always support and show special confidence in the Bodhisattvas.

"World-Honored One, if sons and daughters of good families want to give rise to the highest, most fulfilled, awakened mind, what should they rely on and what should they do to master their thinking?"

The Buddha said to Subhuti, "This is how the Bodhisattva Mahasattvas master their thinking: 'However many species of living beings there are—whether born from eggs, from the womb, from moisture, or spontaneously; whether they have form or do not have form; whether they have perceptions or do not have perceptions; or whether it cannot be said of them that they have perceptions or that they do not have perceptions, we must lead all these beings to nirvana so that they can be liberated. Yet when this innumerable, immeasurable, infinite number of beings has become liberated, we do not, in truth, think that a single being has been liberated.'

"Why is this so? If, Subhuti, a bodhisattva holds on to the idea that a self, a person, a living being, or a life span exists, that person is not a true bodhisattva.

"Moreover, Subhuti, when a bodhisattva practices generosity, she does not rely on any object—any form, sound, smell, taste, tactile object, or dharma—to practice generosity. That, Subhuti, is the spirit in which a bodhisattva practices generosity, not relying on signs. Why? If a bodhisattva practices generosity without relying on signs, the happiness that results cannot be conceived of or measured.

"Subhuti, if a bodhisattva does not rely on any concept while practicing generosity, the happiness that results from that virtuous act is as great as space. It cannot be measured. Subhuti, the bodhisattvas should let their minds dwell in the teachings I have just given.

"Subhuti, a bodhisattva who still depends on notions to practice generosity is like someone walking in the dark. She will not see anything. But when a bodhisattva does not depend on notions to practice generosity, she is like someone with good eyesight walking under the bright light of the sun. She can see all shapes and colors."[*]

Suggested Practice
Stopping

One of the core practices of the Plum Village tradition is

---

[*] Vajracchedika Prajñaparamita (Diamond) Sutra, Taisho Revised Tripitaka 335. See Thich Nhat Hanh, *Chanting from the Heart*.

the practice of stopping. If you visit one of our monasteries, you will discover that every time a bell chimes, whether it is a clock, a monastery bell, or the telephone, we physically stop whatever it is we are doing, gently close our eyes, and enjoy breathing in and out for at least three breaths.

On the surface, stopping seems like a very simple practice; however, it is one of the most powerful—as is often the case with the simplest of practices. Stopping can help us to recognize our patterns, the stories we tell ourselves, and begin to wake up to the strange ways that we try to seek small comforts, rather than seeking the big comfort that we most want, that we most need on a core level.

Create opportunities for stopping this week. When you come back to your breath, you may like to bring awareness to your senses: what you are hearing, what you are seeing, what you are sensing in your body, and so on. Notice whether there are any patterns that emerge. Which of the senses are you naturally drawn to, or is most apparent to you?

CHAPTER THREE

Three Roots and Three Refuges

This morning on the way down to sitting meditation, I was walking through a very thick mist. Often during the winter months here in Deer Park a marine layer settles in overnight and there's a very thick mist that burns off about nine or nine-thirty each morning as the sun begins shining over the peaks of the mountains surrounding the monastery. When I arrived down at the meditation hall, my robes, my hat, and my jacket were all damp from the mist. The mist had permeated the fibers of my clothes, without any effort at all. The mist was just doing what it does and I was just doing what I do, which in this case was walking mindfully to the meditation hall.

When we speak of the Dharma, and the practice of mindfulness, one word that we often use is "permeation." Bringing the energy of awareness and mindfulness to each moment of our life enables that energy to permeate our every action. Every one of our actions and our interactions becomes an opportunity to open our heart, to go more deeply, and to become more fully alive. This is really the essence of Engaged Buddhism in our tradition: using our daily life—using this moment now as our practice—not only the moments that we're on the cushion or when we're doing formal practice.

Can we allow the energy of mindfulness to infuse our lives like tea leaves in hot water? Buddhist monastics are big tea drinkers. There's never an occasion that is too small or too large for a pot of tea. When we make a cup of tea, we place the tea leaves into the teapot and pour boiling water on them. As the tea leaves interact with the water, they release color, fragrance, and taste into the water, infusing the water and changing its nature into tea. Sometimes as I am making tea, I ask myself, at which point does the water stop being referred to as water and begin to be called tea? Many interesting answers can emerge from looking in this way.

The Three Roots

A core concept in Buddhist psychology is that of the Three Roots: greed; hatred or ill will; and ignorance or, as it's sometimes called, delusion. Continuing with the image of permeation, these Three Roots are energies that subtly (or less subtly) permeate our inner being: our perceptions, our motivations, and the ways that we interact with the world around us. One simple way to grasp this concept is to visualize a bowl of clear water in which we drop a drop or two of food coloring. The food coloring permeates all the different molecules in the water and the water becomes the color of the food coloring: it becomes red; it becomes blue; it becomes green. The energies of the Three Roots color our perceptions and consciousness in the same way. We view everything through the "lenses" of the Three Roots.

These Three Roots express themselves differently in each one of us. For some of us one or another of the roots will be deeper or stronger than the others. Each of us has our own unique makeup, and developing a familiarity with the Three Roots can be a very helpful doorway to walk through in terms of recognizing the subtle motivations that pervade our thoughts, our actions, and our words.

1. Greed

The first of the roots that the Buddha described is the root of greed. In the Pali language, greed is called *tanha* or "thirst."

Greed in Buddhist Psychology is based around the idea of always wanting one more thing, never quite being satisfied. As we shared earlier, one of the key practices in the Plum Village tradition is the practice of "I have enough." When we contemplate this root of greed or thirst within us, we recognize a very subtle, unconscious drive in each one of us: the searching after experiences, people, situations, objects that we think are going to take the edge off, that we think are going to make us feel whole.

We grasp onto someone or something—a person, an experience, an idea—that we believe is going to give us the security we so desperately seek. As we bring our awareness to the area of our "thirst," initially we will most probably be more aware of external objects of our grasping. Slowly our awareness begins to illuminate the more subtle realm of internal objects: experiences—both wonderful and less-than wonderful; notions of who we are or who another person is; resentments; and often, what we believe are our attainments in our meditation practice. Bringing awareness to the realm of greed can help us to be able to begin again and again with every breath and to notice our "seeking" mind.

We have this drive where we're looking for something or someone to fill the void that we have, at the same time that there's a subtle knowingness in us which recognizes that the little fix we keep running after is not going to provide us lasting relief.

Once when I was sitting with Thay, he turned to me and shared, "You know, Brother Phap Hai, there is a teaching in Mahayana Buddhism that there is nothing that is not the Dharma, there is nothing that is not a teaching if we are sufficiently aware."

I've really taken those words to heart. We speak a lot about engaged Buddhism and our daily life as our practice. Can we also allow our daily life, our daily experiences to be our teachers as well?

A couple of years ago, I visited my family in Australia. Their neighborhood has a lot of mom-and-pop corner stores. When I was visiting my brother, he asked me whether I would be willing to go down to the store to pick up some milk. I walked the two blocks down to the corner store where I found myself standing behind two very excited young boys who were gazing at the candy counter, enraptured.

These two boys had what for them seemed to be a considerable amount of money—perhaps five dollars—and were chattering about which candies to get. Finally they made their selections, and as the shopkeeper was bagging them up, one of the young boys turned to the other and said excitedly, "Hey, man, we're going to get sick!" The other boy said, "Awesome!" I laughed and caught the eye of the woman behind the counter, and we smiled at each other. This is often our situation: in our heart of hearts we know that certain behaviors are not conducive to that which we are seeking—but goodness, for the first few mouthfuls, those candies are sweet!

In the tender, honest place in our hearts, do we recognize this energy in us too? What are some of the ways that it manifests in you? What are some of the ideas of yourself and others that you are holding on to? What does being a "spiritual practitioner" mean to you? Are there ways in which this idea is an obstacle?

Giving

The practice that the Buddha offered for recognizing and transforming our seeking mind—the mind that's always running after something—is the practice of giving, the giving of material things, the giving of non-fear, and the giving of the Dharma, as well as being generous with our time and our energy.

In the Buddhist tradition, the practice of *dana*, the practice of giving, is one of the very first practices that is taught to somebody who is just encountering the Buddhist path. I love the fact that at the very beginning, we're invited into the concrete practice of opening our hearts and connecting with others. From the very get-go, we build our spiritual life on the foundation of the recognition of our interrelationship with the world around us. We're encouraged to see how our practice is connected with the happiness of others, how our practice is a form of generosity. The practice of dana holds up a very clear mirror in which we can recognize areas of holding back; fears and resistance will definitely arise for us, particularly since embarking on this path brings about a radical reassessment and realignment of the holy trinity that we have taken refuge in up to this point: "I, Me, and My."

An interesting question for us to reflect on is: Is my spiritual practice a form of giving, a form of dana? If so, how? What are the things that are easy for me to give? What are the situations in which it's easy for me to be there with an open heart, an open spirit? And what are the situations and people and places that are difficult for me, where I shut down, even subtly? "Shutting down" here can be shutting down in as subtle a form as thinking, "I'm right and you're wrong," or, "You and me, we're very separate," or, "You have your idea, I have mine."

Our seeking mind is very subtle and we're always running after one thing or another. The mantra "I have enough" that we explored in Chapter one is a really powerful practice for us, to recognize the conditions of happiness, the many ways that we're supported by so many living beings in our lives.

2. Ill Will

The second root that exists very deeply in our consciousness is the root of ill will, which is sometimes referred to as aversion, or hatred. At its most fundamental level, ill will represents a shutting down or a closing down toward other people, toward experiences, and, for most of us, toward ourselves.

Mindfulness

The practice that the Buddha offered for us to work with and explore our root of ill will is the practice of applied mindfulness through the Five Mindfulness Trainings. We see them as gifts we offer to ourselves and to those around us. In fact, there's a text in the Anguttara Nikaya in the Pali Canon that refers to the Five Mindfulness Trainings as "five ancient gifts honored by the wise ones."

How do we approach our own practice of the mindfulness trainings? Do we approach them as gifts, as offerings of self-care and care for others, as ways to open our hearts and help us to recognize behaviors and attitudes that can be harmful to ourselves and to others? Or do we approach them with a subtle spirit of ill will in the sense that they are rules that we judge ourselves by, commandments that we can never quite fulfill? This is a reflection that we can use in our practice, as we move through the day to consider our relationship with the mindfulness trainings.

It may be that as we contemplate our relationship to the mindfulness trainings we have undertaken, we discover that we have different relationships with each of them. Perhaps we relate to some of the mindfulness trainings very openly as gifts and as offerings of the heart, and yet we still relate to others in terms of commandments. The mindfulness trainings are offered in a spirit for us to recognize those places and those situations in which we shut down, in which we behave in a way that harms ourselves as well as others. They are mirrors for us to recognize the multitude of ways in which we choose *not* to care for ourselves and for others, as well as the times we do.

When people hear the term that we use in the Buddhist tradition for the monastic precepts, they're often surprised. We call the monastic precepts the Pratimoksha (Sanskrit) or Patimokkha (Pali). Pratimoksha means "freedom every-where." If you're a student of the Vedic philosophy or Hinduism, you know that *moksha* means liberation, freedom, complete freedom. And *prati* means everywhere: freedom wherever we go. This can sound kind of paradoxical, if we approach the mindfulness trainings from the angle of rules.

If we are able to approach the mindfulness trainings as skillful means that help us to open our heart, that help us to be able to take care of what's arising in our mind, what's arising in our body, what's arising in this moment, then they are great gifts of love. The mindfulness trainings are often referred to also as an expression of awakening itself, that they are the concrete manifestation of the Buddha Body, the *buddhakaya.*

3. Delusion

The third root that exists in our mind to a greater or lesser extent is the root of delusion. Delusion in Buddhist psychology means not seeing things as they really are, being caught by the appearance and not going any deeper than that: you are you, I am I, happiness is happiness, sadness is sadness and never the twain shall meet. This is the kind of attitude that delusion gives rise to. The delusion that we suffer most from is the delusion of separateness.

Meditation

The Buddha offered the practice of *bhavana,* of meditation, of cultivating our mind to develop insight, to be able to see more clearly what's right in front of us or what's arising within us, as a practice to work with our root of delusion.

When we think of an aspiring artist, we're very compassionate toward their efforts when they're just starting out. We know that they need to familiarize themselves with the media that they choose to use; they need to understand which brush to use for what kind of line that they're painting on the canvas. They need to understand how the paints attach to the canvas, how long they take to dry, what kind of images and textures are created with different movements of the hand. It takes time and effort to re-create the image that we're seeing with our physical eyes or indeed our mind's eye on the canvas.

When I was in high school, I took art class for a number of years. At one point we were asked to draw a horse. I spent a lot of effort drawing my horse. I can still see myself bent over the paper with my tongue poking out. When I finished, I thought, "This is really great! Look at the tail flowing out, look at the mane blowing in the breeze; it's almost alive." Then the teacher came around and looked at everybody's drawings. When she got to me and looked over my shoulder, she said, "You were supposed to be drawing a horse! Why did you draw a dog?"

I'm somewhat more humble about my abilities these days, but I enjoyed the process nonetheless, and I'm still a little proud of my drawing even if it doesn't seem to anybody else to be a horse.

Thay has often reminded us that we need to practice meditation like an artist. As artists, we get familiar with our media, we learn how to hold the brush, and choose which paint to use for which image and which emotion we want to express. And we use these tools as well as our own personal life experience to create our painting. And when we look at the great artists, they were using pretty much the same tools as us but the paintings, the images that they came out with are very different. They used the same material in very different ways, according to their own capacities and tendencies.

The life of meditation practice is the same; the manifestation of our practice will be uniquely our own. We all have our own unique strengths and our own unique challenges to work with. As intelligent practitioners, our invitation is to take our lived experience—our most wondrous experiences and darkest sufferings—and allow the practice of mindfulness to root itself in us and express itself through us to permeate our lives. The biggest gift we can offer to ourselves and to our Sangha is the gift of who we really are.

The Three Doors of Liberation

When we speak of the Threes, the third of the Three Doors of Liberation is *wishlessness*. This is the door we walk through when we practice recognizing that we are already that which we want to become. What is it you want to become? Peaceful? Happy? Wealthy?

What is it that we're looking for? As we shared in the previous chapter: Where do we think we're going to find it? Who are we actually—and who is the Buddha anyway? What is my experience of happiness exactly? What is my experience of sadness? What are the ideas that I hold about my happiness and my sadness, about who I am, about who you are?

From exploring those questions—not only as a mental exercise, but through the moment-to-moment application of the contemplation of the Three Roots—a recognition begins to arise, a recognition that they're simply ideas and concepts, not the reality itself. Don't get me wrong: concepts and ideas are important, but they only imperfectly describe reality.

The permeation of the Three Roots in our consciousness is very subtle. As we develop our mindful awareness through the fundamental practices—mindful walking, mindful sitting, mindful eating, inviting the mindfulness trainings into our lives—we become more sensitive and more aware of what's arising in our mind, and we begin to notice the subtle drives, the drives that are motivating our actions, that are perfuming our encounters; they become increasingly apparent to us. Beginning to recognize the functioning of the Three Roots in our daily life is a very important and powerful practice. Are we willing to ask ourselves, "Are we sure?" This is the invitation for this week as we continue on our journey.

The Three Refuges

In Buddhism, we speak of the practice of taking refuge. We take refuge in the Buddha, the Awakened One within us and around us; in the Dharma, the teachings of love and understanding; and in the Sangha. The term Sangha usually refers to our community of practice, but in a broader sense it can also be any supportive condition that helps us to touch the seeds of love and understanding within us.

Although we recite the Three Refuges each day, taking refuge is a moment-by-moment practice, as well as a profound realization.

In the Chinese language, when we speak of taking refuge we don't just say, "I take refuge," but we say, "I return to and I rely upon the Buddha, the Dharma, and the Sangha." I think that is a very helpful framework for us in our own practice of taking refuge. What does it mean to me to return to and rely upon the Sangha—body, speech, and mind? How is my practice of taking refuge a lived reality rather than some formula that I just recite once or twice a day? If we are really honest, many, if not most of us, might recite and have the intention to practice taking refuge in the Sangha, but in fact we take refuge in all the people that we get along with and agree with—but not that person over there who irritates us.

What do you take refuge in? Where do you seek

shelter? There's an easy way to find out. If we begin to pay attention to the habitual thoughts, emotions, and behaviors that manifest in us throughout the day, then we will begin to see clearly that most often we "return and rely" not upon the Buddha, the Dharma, and the Sangha, but rather our anger, resentment, our mistaken perceptions, and the "holy trinity" of I, Me, and My.

Questions for Reflection

1. Reflecting on my practice, how is my practice a gift—to myself, my dear ones, my Sangha?

2. From my practice of stopping and coming back to my senses during the past week—what themes have emerged? Have I noticed that I tend to be more aware of sounds, or smells, or tastes, or sights, or sensations? What are some of the more consistent themes that have been running through my thoughts this past week?

3. Reflecting back over my mandala of practice for this week (study, practice, work, play)—what have I found easy and what have I found challenging? What do I resist most?

Suggested Practice
Stop and Reflect

This coming week, building on the practice of coming back to our senses, throughout the day we are invited to walk through the door of becoming more aware of the three roots in our consciousness—the seeking, grasping mind; aversion; and not seeing things as they are.

Throughout this coming week, in your stopping practice, notice and smile to the stories that you tell yourself about the experiences that you are having. What interpretations of bare experience are you making?

At the end of the week, it may be helpful to go back over the themes that we noticed during the week and see if they still resonate with us or if, a few days later, we see the situation differently.

CHAPTER FOUR

The Four Foundations of Mindfulness

That which we pay attention to grows stronger. In the sutras, again and again, the Buddha taught about the importance of developing appropriate attention: in Sanskrit, *yoniso manaskara*. This is another way of referring to the appropriately directed faculty of mindfulness.

Mindfulness always has an object. We can bring mindful attention to our breath, to our steps, to our emotions, and it can be described as either "appropriate" (*yoniso*) or "not yet appropriate" (*ayoniso*), depending on our motivations and the objects of our attention. I know people who have nurtured the seed of resentment for twenty or more years.

There's one funny story that comes to mind about this. After our parents passed away, my younger brother and I went to live with our grandmother. She was of the old-school style of cooking: three veg and protein, cooked quite plainly. I, on the other hand, have always loved spicy food.

One day, my grandmother was a little tired, so I offered to cook dinner. I decided to cook a green curry, which, I swear, I carefully made as mild as possible. We sat down for dinner and my grandmother took a small bite and started coughing so violently that she had to go over to the sink for a drink of water. She asked me whether I was trying to poison her with chili! I tried to explain that this was a mild version, but having never eaten Thai food, she had a hard time believing the story. For years and years after, at every family gathering, she would tell the story of the time I tried to "poison her with chili." It became a running joke in our family: we all knew that whenever we got together it would only be a matter of time before this story would emerge. You could say that my grandmother was very skilled at keeping this memory alive in all of our minds!

What's the object of our attention and what kind of nourishment is it providing us? What is dominating our attention and where do we choose to put our attention? Our real freedom as human beings is the capacity to choose. We can choose the objects of our attention; we can choose what to nurture in ourselves and in others. Thay often uses the imagery of becoming a skillful gardener. This is what the practice is about. In the Chinese language, we often refer to each other as *dao lu*: Cultivators of the Way. Isn't that a beautiful way to refer to a practitioner?

If you're a cultivator, a gardener—particularly an organic gardener—you know that certain seeds sprout at certain times under certain circumstances. You know that basil, for example, grows in summer. So you don't feel that it is strange or tragic when your tomato plant isn't bearing fruit in the winter. You know which seeds sprout in which conditions, and you develop an awareness of natural cycles and learn to collaborate with them.

Our practice life is a lot like that. Seeds—seeds of love, understanding, compassion, joy—will sprout in their own time and in their own way in each one of us. Depending on a number of factors, the seeds will manifest differently in each one of us, just as a plant can look quite different in different parts of the world. The seed of compassion is going to look a little different in each one of us. The same goes for the seeds of joy, happiness, anger, or depression.

Our meditation practice is the practice of becoming a skillful gardener: creating the best conditions for the most wholesome seeds, the seeds that are most nourishing, to have the conditions to arise and flourish within us and also in those we come into contact with. This is what's meant by yoniso manaskara, appropriate attention—bringing attention to the choices we make to nourish ourselves. We recognize what is in alignment with our deepest aspirations and consciously choose to nurture and nourish those seeds in ourselves as well as in others.

If you are a gardener, then it is important to be able to distinguish the plants from the weeds. You don't want to spend a lot of time and energy in raising a crop of zucchini only to find that when you weeded the garden bed a few weeks ago you pulled out the zucchini plants and have been watering the weeds instead. That's not to say that the weeds do not have their value, because they do. The seeds in our consciousness that we would normally categorize as "negative," such as anger, have their value if we know how to look deeply into them and understand how to channel their energy. The important thing here is intentionality. If you are raising a crop of zucchini, raise a crop of zucchini with all your heart.

We become skillful gardeners for ourselves, first of all, and then for those around us. Our mind is our garden, our Sangha is our garden; our family is our garden.

One of the most foundational Buddhist meditation practices is The Four Frames of Reference, or, as they are more commonly known, The Four Establishments of Mindfulness—the four foundations upon which mindfulness, concentration, and insight are firmly established. Unless we establish our mindfulness upon these four foundations, mindfulness remains just an idea, a concept, rather than a lived experience. Developing mindfulness through these four foundations develops our capacity to be fully present and to become more skillful with regard to appropriate attention.

1. Awareness of Body

The first establishment of mindfulness is *mindfulness of the body in the body*. I love the phrasing of this. It's not mindfulness of the body from two inches away; it is mindfulness of the body from within the body, from the very heart of our experience. For many of us, we're separated somewhat from our physicality, and the practice of mindfulness of the body from within the body is an incredibly healing practice. Our practice brings us down from above our ears into the core of our embodied experience. As our mindful attention develops, it deepens into concentration, which in Buddhism means to be one with the object of our attention, the observer and the observed becoming one.

So how do we begin to establish mindfulness of the body in the body? We have already discovered our breath and are developing some intimacy with it as a meditation object, both in sitting meditation and throughout the day. One way to begin establishing our mindful attention within our body is to bring awareness to our body as we move through the four positions of standing, walking, sitting, and lying down.

We bring our mindful awareness to each of these positions of our body by noting, for example, "I am standing," and really experiencing what it is to stand. What does it feel like? What sensations arise? Carry this spacious awareness through the day. If we are new to this practice, it will be challenging to maintain awareness constantly, so we might want to begin by simply noting whenever we change our posture. When you move from standing to sitting, you can note to yourself, "sitting," and take a split second to be aware that you're sitting, rooting yourself in your body. When you lie down, just note to yourself, "lying down." When walking, bring awareness to your body in motion and the simple fact that you're walking—what a joy!

I love to watch people practice walking meditation for the first time or for the first few times. We think we know what it is to walk: we think we learned it all when we were toddlers. Nothing new here! We think we know how our feet move, how our body moves through space. When people first begin to slow down and take three steps with their in-breath, three steps with their out-breath, oftentimes it can be a very strange experience for them and they start to feel off balance and teeter around a little bit because they're so habituated to a particular unconscious way of walking. There is so much to discover even in the simplest, most ordinary actions, or perhaps I should say *especially* in the simplest, most ordinary actions.

In the same way we think that we already know what it is to sit and to lie down. We think we know what it is to stand. Mindfulness of the body is a practice of discovery of the habitual ways we go about moving our bodies, of interacting with space; it's a practice of unlearning and relearning. There are so many discoveries awaiting you when you return to intimacy with your body, just as it is. There are so many "aha" moments. Your body is such a wonder, even with its aches and pains and love handles and gray hair (or, as I have heard them called, *wisdom strands*).

As our body-based awareness grows and develops we notice all the subtle movements of the muscles. We even begin to notice the intention to move. We notice the arising and passing away of sensations in each moment. Mindfulness of the body can be very profound. To begin to develop this first foundation of mindfulness, begin by simply noting the different positions of your body as you move into them with that kind, relaxed, and gentle awareness that we call mindfulness.

Suggested Practice
Body Scan

Another practice of mindfulness of the body in the body is to do a complete body scan. We can do this during sitting meditation or at other points during the day. We can be aware of all the different parts of our body; traditionally there are thirty-two listed: *hair of the head, hair of the body, nails, teeth, skin, muscle, tendons, bones, bone marrow, spleen, heart, liver, membranes, kidneys, lungs, large intestines, small intestines, gorge, feces, gall, phlegm, lymph, blood, sweat, fat, tears, oil, saliva, mucus, oil in the joints, urine, brain.*

As you've begun to discover in this book, Buddhism is very big on lists. There are lists of everything, primarily because Buddhism was an oral tradition for approximately five hundred years after the Buddha's passing. So it was a great way for people to memorize. There's a profound oral lineage in the Buddhist teachings.

Concretely, when we practice the body scan, we flow our mindful attention through the different parts of our body: hair on the head, hair on the body, nails, our teeth, our skin, our heart, our blood, our lungs, our intestines, our bones, our bone marrow, all the different parts of our body, and recognize them for what they are, bringing the energy of mindful awareness there. When we bring the energy of mindfulness to an organ, a tissue, or a part of our body—for me at least—gratitude arises.

Speaking of hair on the head, as a monk I don't have that much. Last year I was sitting on the train in Brisbane in front of two young commuters talking to each other on their way to work. One of the guys complained to the other, "Dude, I'm having such a bad-hair day, I just can't get it to look right today."

I sat there and realized that one of the great happinesses of monastic life is that I never have bad-hair days. I do, however, have to be completely honest and share that every single day of my life I have a no-hair day!

Suggested Practice
Total Relaxation

One way that we practice scanning our body in our Plum Village tradition is total relaxation—taking some time during our workday or at the end of the day to lie down and do a full body scan, recognizing, relaxing, and releasing all the different parts of the body.

The Buddha gave a very striking image in the Discourse on the Four Establishments of Mindfulness when speaking about establishing mindfulness of the body in the body. He said, "Scan your body just like a farmer goes through a bag of mixed seeds and says, 'This is a sesame seed, this is a rice grain, these are mungbeans.'" Recognize all the different parts of your body in that way, just as the farmer in the example separates out the different types of seeds.

As we scan our body, we send a lot of love to the different organs in the different parts of our body. We tend to judge ourselves so harshly. We've bought into the belief that we have been fed by the media, by society, or sometimes by our loved ones that we're not beautiful just as we are.

Will you allow yourself to come back home to your body and to send loving kindness to every cell, every tissue, every organ, and every single part of yourself unconditionally?

A story that a practitioner told me in 1998 continues to live on in me all of these years later. She shared how a teacher came into the classroom one morning and greeted the class: "Good morning, class," and the class said, "Good morning, Miss." Then one little boy shouted out, "Miss, Miss, you're looking really ugly today!" The teacher breathed in and out for a moment and, thanks to her practice of sending loving kindness to all the different parts of her body, instead of anger, she felt a sense of spaciousness emerge from within her. She turned around to him and said, "You know, when I looked in the mirror this morning and saw my face staring back at me, I thought so too, but all in all, I'm pretty happy the way I am."

Suggested Practice
Sangha Body

Another aspect of establishing mindfulness of the body is the teaching in the Plum Village tradition that our community of practice, our Sangha, is our body—we call it our Sangha body. As we go through the different parts in our body we might like to also go through the different parts that make up the body of our Sangha, recognizing them for what they are: this person is a kidney bean, this person is a rice grain, this person is a sesame seed. Recognize each person for what they are and consider how they enrich your life, even if the "enrichment" may not be what you normally look for. How do they help you grow, how do they contribute to your transformation? How are you a supportive condition for them? Can you see the Sangha body as your body? Can you return to and rely upon your Sangha body?

Suggested Practice
Elements in the Body

Another practice that the Buddha offered for developing awareness of the body is to be aware of the four great elements that make up our body. I remember when I was practicing Vipassana meditation in Sri Lanka, we were offered the following powerful meditation on the four elements in the body. Having established mindfulness in our body, we contemplate the four elements:

1. The fire element is heat, warmth, and also the motivation that drives us; it is also our metabolism. Contemplate how the fire element manifests in your body.

2. The earth element is all the things that are solid, all the things we can touch, the firm parts (or, as we get older, the less firm parts of our body).

3. The water element is all the fluids in our body: blood, the synovial fluid, the urine, the bile, all the different liquids that make up our body.

4. The air element is the space in our body, also the air that enters and leaves our body, our breath, and so forth. The air element is also the movement that our body makes.

Suggested Practice

Mindfulness of Breathing

In our tradition, we emphasize mindfulness of breathing for the practice of the mindfulness of the air element within us, and entering and leaving our body. It's something that's very easy and concrete to be in contact with.

Our breath is never the same from one moment to the next; every breath is a new beginning and an ending. If you were not a practitioner of meditation, it would be easy to think that following your breathing would be incredibly boring, kind of like watching paint dry or grass grow. But in fact the breath keeps changing all the time and gets subtler and subtler and subtler. It's a very profound practice. For the record, before moving on I have to say that recently I've found that there's nothing wrong with sitting and enjoying paint drying or grass growing. Why are we always in such a hurry? What else do we think we need to do in this moment? The paint drying and the grass growing symbolize all of the "mundane" and "everyday" aspects of our life that we normally try to get over and done with so that we can do "something meaningful." This reminds me of the beautiful poem by Basho: "Sitting quietly, doing nothing, Spring comes and the grass grows by itself." * The real practice begins when the absolutely mundane, the absolutely ordinary become sacred experiences.

Take some time now to reconnect with your breath. As your breath naturally flows in, note "in," as it flows out, note "out." When you feel yourself present with your breath and in your body, continue on with a few more exercises:

Breathing in, I experience the full length of my in-breath.

Breathing out, I experience the full length of my

---

* From the Zenrin Kushu, cited in Alan Watts, *The Way of Zen* (New York: Vintage, 1999), 134.

out-breath.

With my in-breath, what is it that I'm bringing into my consciousness this moment?

As I breathe out, what is it that I'm offering at this moment?

2. Awareness of Feelings

The second establishment of mindfulness is awareness of the *feelings in the feelings*. As we become grounded in the lived experience of our body, we start to notice and become more intimate with sensations arising, being there for a period of time, and passing away in our body. As we become increasingly aware of the sensations in our body, we become aware of the feelings and emotions that are manifesting in our consciousness. Often we will notice that emotion is very deeply related to sensations in the body. Feelings and emotions are arising and being with us for a period of time and then passing away almost constantly. Often this is described as the river of feelings. When we work with this establishment of mindfulness, we begin to become aware of and name the feelings that are arising. When we come into contact with sense objects, when we come into contact with an experience—whether it's something a person said or a smell or a sensation or a taste—a feeling is arising that we call by its name.

In the beginning, we might just feel a sensation or something arising, and we don't yet have a vocabulary for it. As we develop our attention, we get more and more familiar with what feelings are arising, and we develop the language, the vocabulary, to call them by their true names. "This is joy arising, this is happiness arising, this is sadness, this is jealousy." We recognize each emotion for what it is and we don't get carried away by strong emotions. Thay calls this practice "smiling to what's arising."

Whatever is arising is okay; we accept it as it is. In that spacious acceptance, we don't get carried away by strong emotions. All our lives, we've been carried away by this emotion and that emotion; we've been swinging like a pendulum. There are times that the river of emotions can feel like a raging torrent. When we develop mindful awareness, we recognize what this experience feels like in our body, in our mind, how it's expressing itself in this moment. As we develop this skill, we discover that we have the capacity to take good care of the emotion or feeling that's arising. We approach it as a teacher; we invite and welcome the teaching that it has for us.

What do those emotions that I normally label as "negative" have to teach me? What do those emotions that I normally label as "positive" have to teach me? Feelings in Buddhist psychology are normally divided into three categories: pleasant, painful, and a third category that we call "neither pleasant nor painful." Let's simplify this third category it by calling it "neutral."

As a beginner in bringing awareness to the realm of feelings, we tend to be only aware of the feelings or emotions that arise at either end of the pendulum swing, the big, showy, neon-Vegas-light ones, like happiness, sadness, rage, all of the really strong emotions. Over time, as we develop more sensitive awareness and more intimate familiarity with what's taking place within us, we notice more and more subtle feelings and emotions that are arising; particularly we begin to notice those feelings that are called "neutral." They are very subtle indeed.

3. Awareness of Mind

In the Vijñanavada (Mind Only) school of Buddhist psychology, fifty-one seeds are described as being present in our consciousness in latent form. Feeling is one of the fifty-one seeds, and the remaining fifty are what we refer to as the third establishment of mindfulness, which is *awareness of mind in the mind.* [*]

In this establishment of mindfulness we develop

---

[*] For a more detailed discussion of the fifty-one mental formations, please see Thich Nhat Hanh, *Understanding our Mind* (Berkeley, CA: Parallax Press, 2006).

awareness of what are called *mental formations.* A simple way of understanding mental formation is to understand that all things are formations made up of many different parts. Emotions are formations, feelings are formations, but there are formations that are not necessarily primarily in the feeling arena, and this is what we're referring to in the third establishment of mindfulness.

Some mental formations are called "universal," which means that they're always there: contact, attention, feeling, perception, and volition; volition means that which drives us forward. Some of the formations in our mind arise only under particular circumstances, like wisdom, or determination, or mindfulness. So we can see here that mindfulness is not a feeling. There are mental formations that are wholesome, there are also mental formations that are unwholesome, some that are sometimes one way and sometimes another. As we practice with this establishment of mindfulness, we start to notice the frames, the flavors, that are in our mind, the frames that give rise to the feelings and emotions that we're experiencing.

4. Awareness of Objects of Mind

The fourth foundation of mindfulness is *mindfulness of the objects of mind in the objects of mind.* Earlier I shared that mindfulness always has an object: When we're mindful, we're always mindful of something or someone. There has to be an object. This is what we're talking about when we're talking about being mindful of the objects of mind in the objects of mind. If we're angry, we're angry with someone or something. If we're happy, we're happy with something or someone. There's always an object. This establishment of mindfulness is bringing awareness to those objects that bring themselves to our mind's attention, those objects that are the stimulus for some feeling, emotion, or mental formation to arise—recognizing what's there in front of our eyes, in front of the doorways of our perception.

Suggested Practice
Four Noble Messengers

When we consider the story of the Buddha, the prince who lived in a castle sheltered from the world and who then found his way out of the castle into the forest to embark on a journey of awakening, it is of course the story of somebody who lived 2,600-odd years ago. But if we are willing to look more deeply, it also mirrors our own story.

Let us consider our own situations. For much of my life I ran away from my experience and I didn't want to look at it. I was afraid of it somehow. And then at certain points in my life I was touched; something pierced through the big walls that I built around myself. We give a name to this kind of piercing experience that leaves a deep impression: a noble messenger. In the Buddha's story there were four noble messengers that pierced his consciousness and moved him forward on his path. He saw someone who was old, he saw someone who was sick, he saw someone who was dead, and finally he saw a spiritual practitioner, an ascetic in the forest.

Who or what are your noble messengers? What invited you to embark upon this journey of opening your heart, of understanding your experience? This is a very important aspect that I felt invited to share when I was thinking about the Four. You might discover that you have less than four or more than four. Maybe you have twenty noble messengers! Take some time this week to consider and honor the journey that you have made to be where you are in this moment.

Reading

Selection from the Satipatthana Sutra on the Four Establishments of Mindfulness

---

~ I ~

I heard these words of the Buddha one time when he was living at Kammassadhamma, a market town of the Kuru people. The Buddha addressed the bhikkhus, "O bhikkhus."

And the bhikkhus replied, "Venerable."

The Buddha said, "Bhikkhus, there is a most wonderful way to help living beings realize purification, overcome directly grief and sorrow, end pain and anxiety, travel the right path, and realize nirvana. This way is the Four Establishments of Mindfulness.

"What are the Four Establishments?

1. "Bhikkhus, a practitioner remains established in the observation of the body in the body, diligent, with clear understanding, mindful, having abandoned every craving and every distaste for this life.

2. "He remains established in the observation of the feelings in the feelings, diligent, with clear understanding, mindful, having abandoned every craving and every distaste for this life.

3. "He remains established in the observation of the mind in the mind, diligent, with clear understanding, mindful, having abandoned every craving and every distaste for this life.

4. "He remains established in the observation of the objects of mind in the objects of mind, diligent, with clear understanding, mindful, having abandoned every craving and every distaste for this life."

~ II ~

"And how does a practitioner remain established in the observation of the body in the body?

"She goes to the forest, to the foot of a tree, or to an empty room, sits down cross-legged in the lotus position, holds her body straight, and establishes mindfulness in front of her. She breathes in, aware that she is breathing in. She breathes out, aware that she is breathing out. When she breathes in a long breath, she knows, 'I am breathing in a long breath.' When she breathes out a long breath, she knows, 'I am breathing out a long breath.'

"When she breathes in a short breath, she knows, 'I am breathing in a short breath.'

"When she breathes out a short breath, she knows, 'I am breathing out a short breath.'

"She uses the following practice: 'Breathing in, I am aware of my whole body. Breathing out, I am aware of my whole body. Breathing in, I calm my body. Breathing out, I calm my body.'

"Just as a skilled potter knows when he makes a long turn on the wheel, 'I am making a long turn,' and knows when he makes a short turn, 'I am making a short turn,' so a practitioner, when she breathes in a long breath, knows, 'I am breathing in a long breath,' and when she breathes in a short breath, knows, 'I am breathing in a short breath,' when she breathes out a long breath, knows, 'I am breathing out a long breath,' and when she breathes out a short breath, knows, 'I am breathing out a short breath.'

"She uses the following practice: 'Breathing in, I am aware of my whole body. Breathing out, I am aware of my whole body. Breathing in, I calm my body. Breathing out, I calm my body.'

"Moreover, when a practitioner walks, he is aware, 'I am walking.' When he is standing, he is aware, 'I am standing.' When he is sitting, he is aware, 'I am sitting.' When he is lying down, he is aware, 'I am lying down.' In whatever position his body happens to be, he is aware of the position of his body.

"Moreover, when the practitioner is going forward or backward, he applies full awareness to his going forward or backward. When he looks in front or looks behind, bends down or stands up, he also applies full awareness to what he is doing. He applies full awareness to wearing the sanghati robe or carrying the alms bowl. When he eats or drinks, chews, or savors the food, he applies full awareness to all this. When passing excrement or urinating, he applies full awareness to this. When he walks, stands, lies down, sits, sleeps or wakes up, speaks or is silent, he shines his awareness on all this.

"Further, the practitioner meditates on her very own

body from the soles of the feet upward and then from the hair on top of the head downward, a body contained inside the skin and full of all the impurities which belong to the body: 'Here is the hair of the head, the hairs on the body, the nails, teeth, skin, flesh, sinews, bones, bone marrow, kidneys, heart, liver, diaphragm, spleen, lungs, intestines, bowels, excrement, bile, phlegm, pus, blood, sweat, fat, tears, grease, saliva, mucus, synovial fluid, urine.'

"Bhikkhus, imagine a sack which can be opened at both ends, containing a variety of grains—brown rice, wild rice, mung beans, kidney beans, sesame, white rice. When someone with good eyesight opens the bags, he will review it like this: 'This is brown rice, this is wild rice, these are mung beans, these are kidney beans, these are sesame seeds, this is white rice.' Just so the practitioner passes in review the whole of his body from the soles of the feet to the hair on the top of the head, a body enclosed in a layer of skin and full of all the impurities which belong to the body: 'Here is the hair of the head, the hairs on the body, nails, teeth, skin, flesh, sinews, bones, bone marrow, kidneys, heart, liver, diaphragm, spleen, lungs, intestines, bowels, excrement, bile, phlegm, pus, blood, sweat, fat, tears, grease, saliva, mucus, synovial fluid, urine.'

"Further, in whichever position her body happens to be, the practitioner passes in review the elements which constitute the body: 'In this body is the earth element, the water element, the fire element, and the air element.'

"As a skilled butcher or an apprentice butcher, having killed a cow, might sit at the crossroads to divide the cow into many parts, the practitioner passes in review the elements which comprise her very own body: 'Here in this body are the earth element, the water element, the fire element, and the air element.'...

"This is how the practitioner remains established in the observation of the body in the body, observation of the body from within or from without, or both from within or from without. He remains established in the observation of the process of coming-to-be in the body or the process of dissolution in the body or both in the process of coming-to-be and the process of dissolution. Or he is mindful of the fact, 'There is a body here,' until understanding and full awareness come about. He remains established in the observation, free, not caught in any worldly consideration. That is how to practice observation of the body in the body, O bhikkhus."

~III~

"Bhikkhus, how does a practitioner remain established in the observation of the feelings in the feelings?

"Whenever the practitioner has a pleasant feeling, she is aware, 'I am experiencing a pleasant feeling.' The practitioner practices like this for all the feelings, whether they are pleasant, painful, or neutral, observing when they belong to the body and when they belong to the mind.

"This is how the practitioner remains established in the observation of the feelings in the feelings, observation of the feelings from within or from without, or observation of the feelings both from within and from without. She remains established in the observation of the process of coming-to-be in the feelings or the process of dissolution in the feelings or both in the process of coming-to-be and the process of dissolution. Or she is mindful of the fact, 'There is feeling here,' until understanding and full awareness come about. She remains established in the observation, free, not caught in any worldly consideration. That is how to practice observation of the feelings in the feelings, O bhikkhus."

~IV~

"Bhikkhus, how does a practitioner remain established in the observation of the mind in the mind?

"When his mind is desiring, the practitioner is aware, 'My mind is desiring.' When his mind is not desiring, he is aware, 'My mind is not desiring.' He is aware in the same way concerning a hating mind, a confused mind, a collected mind, a dispersed mind, an expansive mind, a narrow mind, the highest mind, and a concentrated and liberated mind.

"This is how the practitioner remains established in

the observation of the mind in the mind, observation of the mind from within or from without, or observation of the mind both from within and from without. He remains established in the observation of the process of coming-to-be in the mind or the process of dissolution in the mind or both in the process of coming-to-be and the process of dissolution. Or he is mindful of the fact, 'There is mind here,' until understanding and full awareness come about. He remains established in the observation, free, not caught in any worldly consideration. This is how to practice observation of the mind in the mind, O bhikkhus."

~V~

"Bhikkhus, how does a practitioner remain established in the observation of the objects of mind in the objects of mind?

"First of all, she observes the objects of mind in the objects of mind with regard to the Five Hindrances. How does she observe this?

"When sensual desire is present in her, she is aware, 'Sensual desire is present in me.' Or when sensual desire is not present in her, she is aware, 'Sensual desire is not present in me.' When sensual desire begins to arise, she is aware of it. When sensual desire that has already arisen is abandoned, she is aware of it. When sensual desire that has already been abandoned will not arise again in the future, she is aware of it.

"She practices in the same way concerning anger, dullness and drowsiness, agitation and remorse, and doubt.

"Further, the practitioner observes the objects of mind in the objects of mind with regard to the Five Aggregates of Clinging. How does she observe this?

"She observes like this:'Such is form. Such is the arising of form. Such is the disappearance of form. Such is feeling. Such is the arising of feeling.

"Such is the disappearance of feeling. Such is perception. Such is the arising of perception. Such is the disappearance of perception. Such are mental formations. Such is the arising of mental formations. Such is the disappearance of mental formations.

"Such is consciousness. Such is the arising of consciousness. Such is the disappearance of consciousness.

"Further, bhikkhus, the practitioner observes the objects of mind in the objects of mind with regard to the six sense organs and the six sense objects. How does she observe this?

"She is aware of the eyes and aware of the form, and she is aware of the internal formations which are produced in dependence on these two things. She is aware of the birth of a new internal formation and is aware of abandoning an already produced internal formation, and she is aware when an already abandoned internal formation will not arise again.

"She is aware in the same way of the ears and sound, the nose and smell, the tongue and taste, the body and touch, the mind and objects of mind....

"This is how the practitioner remains established in the observation of the objects of mind in the objects of mind either from within or from without, or both from within and from without. She remains established in the observation of the process of coming-to-be in any of the objects of mind or the process of dissolution in the objects of mind or both in the process of coming-to-be and the process of dissolution. Or she is mindful of the fact, 'There is an object of mind here,' until understanding and full awareness come about. She remains established in the observation, free, not caught in any worldly consideration. That is how to practice observation of the objects of mind in the objects of mind, O bhikkhus."

~VI~

"Bhikkhus, he or she who practices the Four Establishments of Mindfulness for seven years can expect one of two fruits—the highest understanding in this very life or, if there remains some residue of affliction, he or she can attain the fruit of no-return.

"Let alone seven years, bhikkhus, whoever practices the Four Establishments of Mindfulness for six, five, four, three, two years or one year, for seven, six, five, four, three, or two months, one month or half a month, can also expect one of two fruits—either the highest understanding in this very life or, if there remains some residue of affliction, he can attain the fruit of no-return.

"That is why we said that this path, the path of the four grounds for the establishment of mindfulness, is the most wonderful path, which helps beings realize purification, transcend grief and sorrow, destroy pain and anxiety, travel the right path, and realize nirvana."

The bhikkhus were delighted to hear the teaching of the Buddha. They took it to heart and began to put it into practice. *

Questions for Reflection

1. Looking back over my own journey of practice, what were the moments, situations, or people that were my noble messengers?

2. What, for me, does it mean to take refuge in the Sangha?

3. What, for me, does it mean to take refuge in myself?

---

* Satipatthana Sutta, Majjhima Nikaya 10. See Thich Nhat Hanh, *Chanting from the Heart.*

4. What, for me, does it mean to look at my Sangha as my body? Just as a body, my Sangha has needs—how do I respond to those?

Suggested Practice

Be Mindful of the Body in the Body

---

1. Practice mindfulness of the body in the body this week—in terms of the four main positions of the body as well as developing awareness of the different parts of the body.

2. Make time this week for body scanning and total relaxation—either a minute here and there throughout the day, or in the evening before going to bed.

CHAPTER FIVE

The Five Trees

As I sit here this morning, my thoughts travel back to
December 2012, when the world was supposed to end. Do
you remember that? It seems that there is always someone
telling us that the world is coming to an end, isn't there? I
remember another time that a preacher predicted that the
world was going to end in May 2011. I went outside, waited
for the world to end, and then went inside and had dinner.

What is "the world" and what is a beginning or an
ending? Is something ever completely over? In Buddhist
contemplation we understand that each moment gives rise
to the next, that this is because that is. We do not exist in
isolation; there is nothing that exists by itself alone.

When I hear "the end of the world," and contemplate
beginnings and endings, I'm always reminded of the verse
in the Buddhist text that "the world exists within our own
mind, within our own body."

There was once a king who called a meeting of the wise people in the kingdom and said, "I want you to gather all knowledge together so that my children can read it and learn." The wise ones went away and came back a year later with over twenty volumes of knowledge. The king looked through the volumes and said, "No, it's too long. Make it shorter." So the wise ones went off and came back in another year with a single volume. The king again rejected it, saying, "No, it's still too long." So once again, the wise ones went off for another year. When they came back to the palace, they handed the king a piece of paper with a single sentence on it that read, "This too shall pass."*

There are times when we are told by others that the world is going to end; there are many more times when we tell ourselves that "this will be the end," whether of a relationship, a feeling, an experience, or a life. The concept that we hold of an absolute beginning of something that can be pinpointed in time, "birth," and an absolute ending, a time when it is all over, "death" or "annihilation," is a big root of many of our most deeply held fears.

Birth and death, coming and going, here and there: all of these concepts exist within our own mind and body. Even

---

* Adapted from: A. J. Jacobs, *The Know-It-All: One Man's Humble Quest to Become the Smartest Person in the World* (New York: Simon and Schuster, 2004) 91.

the simplest thing such as a thought or a mental formation arises, dwells through a period of time, and then seems to pass away. The same is true with our breath: the breath has a moment of beginning, and it has a moment that seems to be a moment of ending. But the ending of a breath gives rise to the next one. The ending of this moment is the birth of the next moment. Life is filled with beginnings and endings, births and deaths, befores and afters: this is reality. But it's only one side of reality; it is conventional truth, but not absolute truth.

When we experience something that is supposedly ending, do we have the capacity to ask ourselves what it might be the beginning of? What is it an invitation into?

The Five Skandhas

One of the most fundamental ways that we view ourselves, our being, is through the framework of the Five Skandhas.*
The Sanskrit word *skandha* is a Sanskrit word that literally means "piles," "heaps," "formations," or "aggregates." These are aspects of our being that depend on each other and together make up that which we commonly refer to as "ourselves" or "me." The Five Skandhas are form, feeling, perception, mental formations, and consciousness.

---

* Red Pine, *The Heart Sutra* (Berkeley, CA: Counterpoint Press, 2005).

In his wonderful book, *The Heart Sutra*, the scholar Red Pine offers us a beautiful way of understanding the concept and the interrelationship of the Five Skandhas. He reminds us that the Sanskrit word *skandha* also means "tree." Consider for a moment a grove of fig trees. Over the course of many years, the trunks and the branches intertwine and become indistinguishable from each other. Just like a grove of fig trees, the skandhas are interrelated, depend on each other, and are separate in name only.

The first skandha, *rupa* or form, is one aspect part of the Two—mind and body (*nama rupa*) mentioned earlier. It refers to our body, our physicality: that which we consider solid and appears firm. I don't know about you, but as I get older I am noticing that my body is beginning to appear less firm in places that it once was, and firm in places that were once loose and limber! So our form, which seems so fixed, is actually always changing over time.

Suggested Practice

Awareness with Closed Eyes

Close your eyes gently and allow yourself to arrive in your body. Feel the sensation of your body pressing against the cushion or the chair that you are sitting in, and also notice the spaces where your body is not touching anything. Begin to notice any sensations that arise in your body—tingling, itching, prickling, tightness, relaxation. You may notice your heartbeat. Observe and rest with these sensations for a few minutes. Notice how sensations and your experience of your body changes from moment to moment.

Collectively the other four skandhas—feeling, perception, mental formations, and consciousness—are what we call mind (nama). When we speak of "mind" in Buddhism or in Buddhist psychology, in simple terms we're speaking of feeling, perception, mental formations, and consciousness.

It is important to understand that the skandhas inter-are, they are not separate entities. Your body is not separate from your mind, from your feeling, or from your perception. If you are angry, for example, it doesn't just exist in your mind alone, it has a measurable physical effect. You feel your muscles tighten and your adrenaline pumping through your body. Emotions, feelings, and thoughts have measurable physical effects. We all grew up hearing things such as "you are what you eat." We discovered in the previous chapter that consciousness is a form of food, nutriment. Therefore it is equally valid to say, "we are what we think."

To give another example of the interrelationship between the five skandhas, at this moment in time you are either reading these words through the physical organs called your eyes, hearing them in audio form, or reading these words through Braille and your sense of touch. When consciousness based on our physical eyes (eye-consciousness) comes in contact with a stimulus—like these words—then a perception is formed (we see something), feeling arises (maybe we like it, maybe we don't), and a mental formation manifests. Similarly when we come in contact with a sound, touch, smell, and thought, we form a perception, and feelings arise, followed by judgment of whether the feeling is pleasant, unpleasant, or neutral. If we begin to contemplate our experience in this way, we begin to understand that we are also co-creating the object of our perception.

A perception is not something that is separate from our body or mental formations and consciousness. Everything is interrelated. Before we enter the door of meditation deeply, we are very sure that we perceive the world fully, completely, and correctly—and that everyone else views the world the same way we do.

A few years ago, I was welcoming some new sisters and brothers of Vietnamese origin to Deer Park. Upon meeting them, one of the young sisters came up close to me, peered into my eyes, and said, "Brother Phap Hai, I have brown eyes, you have green eyes. Do you see the same things I do?"

I would have to say no, we do not experience the same thing that anyone else has experienced. Everything comes through filters and we see an image that we ourselves have created. It is very rare that we perceive something just as it is.

The Buddha taught us that all of our perceptions are wrong or incomplete—there's always more to discover. There is a very profound and straightforward teaching in the Pali canon that acts as an invitation to observe the interpretations that we make of the objects of our perception (or, as I like to put it, the stories we tell ourselves).

At one time a practitioner called Bahiya approached the Buddha and asked for a teaching. The Buddha shared, "When you see something, just see it. When you hear something, just hear it, when you taste something, just taste it ... when you simply [experience] something and don't have any 'therefore,' suffering ends."*

The Five Hindrances

When we begin to practice meditation, we often feel like somebody who has stepped into a river that is like a raging torrent filled with logs and debris. The strong current keeps sweeping us against the direction we want to go and also pulling us under the water from time to time. The Buddha described very clearly five hindrances to our being able to swim up that river, five hindrances to our meditation.

---

* "Bahiya Sutta: About Bahiya" (Udana 1.10), translated from the Pali by John D. Ireland. *Access to Insight* (Legacy Edition), 13 June 2010.

1. Sensual Desire

The first hindrance is sensual desire in the sense of our mind always searching outside of itself and never feeling fulfilled—running after the honey on the edge of the razor blade, that one thing or person outside of ourselves that we think is going to fix us. In a sense, the first hindrance can be understood as always running—running in the mind and in the body. Practicing stopping, coming back, and recognizing what we have available to us right now is a great antidote for our continual searching around for one more thing.

2. Ill Will

The second of the Five Hindrances is ill will. This is ill will toward others and toward ourself. There are times when we approach our meditation practice with a very subtle sense of ill will also. "Ugh! It's time for sitting meditation," or, "Let me just grit my teeth and I'll get through it because I have to do it," or even more subtly, "I am broken and I need to be fixed." The antidote for ill will when it manifests in our mind, is the practice of loving kindness, the practice of inclusiveness.

3. Sloth and Torpor

There are two words used here that comprise this single third hindrance; one is *sloth* and the other one is *torpor*.

They refer to a mental haze and a physical exhaustion that emerges seemingly for no reason. This is not the normal kind of physical and mental exhaustion we feel after a day of work, but this is a resistance, a hindrance that can arise when we begin to focus more on training our monkey mind. We suddenly feel so tired we can hardly move; our mind is so foggy, we need to just lie there and not do anything at all. The Buddha was asked about this situation and he responded in a humorous way. He said, "If, when you're walking you notice sloth and torpor arising, you should practice sitting. If you notice it when you are sitting, practice lying down and go through all the different parts of your body. If you're still tired, you should dwell in the perception of light."

You know, usually we can't fall asleep in a really bright room; this is what the Buddha meant when he invited us to dwell in the perception of light.

"If all that fails, then you'd better just go to sleep with your mind firmly fixed on waking up soon."

4. Restlessness and Remorse

The fourth hindrance is restlessness and remorse. Restlessness is restlessness of body and mind, not being able to settle down. We feel as if we have ants kind of running through our mind, running through our body, running through our thoughts.

Remorse is another aspect of ill will, feeling not good enough, or feeling that we've failed and beating ourselves up about something that we cannot change at this moment in time.

I can't emphasize enough the importance of rejoicing in our own positive and wholesome actions and rejoicing in the wholesome actions of others. The practice of rejoicing, recognizing our own innate goodness and the innate goodness in others, is a powerful antidote to remorse and is really quite delightful. There are times when remorse can be a great teacher, a helpful spur to growth. But for many of us, rather than being a growth experience, it becomes a heavy weight that we carry around and that saps our energy with thoughts of "shoulda, woulda, coulda."

When you notice restlessness arising, first of all identify whether the restlessness is predominantly in your body or predominantly in your mind. If it's predominantly in your body, often it can be from an excess of energy and it might be good to do some physical activity to be able to channel this energy. If it's in your mind you might want to see again where you've been putting your attention through the day. What happened to you that day? What is it that's niggling at you?

5. Skeptical Doubt

The fifth hindrance is skeptical doubt. It's important to ask questions and hold your own experience as preeminent. But skeptical doubt here is a kind of cynicism that can settle over our minds. When we're cynical, often we're stepping back from our experience. There's a sense of shutting ourselves down, of saying no to life.

The Five Faculties

Our mind is dominated by the hindrances mentioned above to different degrees of subtlety. If we are able to remain steadfast and continue our steady mindfulness practice, five beautiful qualities of mind begin to manifest. It is important to recall this when we feel discouraged by raging torrents of negativity.

These five qualities that we have in our mind are described as "faculties" or "capacities." We all have them—yes, even you! As we develop more awareness of our mental formations and emotions, we become more skillful at recognizing these capacities within ourselves: faith, diligence, mindfulness, concentration, and wisdom. As they become more established and present in our minds and in our experience, they transform from mere faculties or capacities into actual strengths or powers.

1. Faith

The first of the five faculties is faith. Faith, in Buddhism, is not the kind of faith that we're used to hearing about in the Christian tradition in the West, where we're used to hearing aphorisms such as "faith is a belief in things not seen." In Buddhism there's a very different approach to the whole aspect of faith. Faith is confidence born of our own lived experience of transformation and also confidence that this path, this journey, has been walked by others, that we can have confidence in the journey of transformation that we ourselves are making.

In the verses on Recollection of the Dharma, the Dharma is described as being "immediately useful and effective." It's not described as being effective only after one month of use, or effective only after ten years of hard labor and hard practice, but *immediately* useful and effective. Our teacher describes this in very simple language as, "If you want peace, peace is with you immediately." If we practice walking meditation and we begin to feel a relief, then we know we're practicing correctly.

Faith is having confidence in the transformation that you're experiencing, confidence in your own capacity to wake up. Yes, believe it or not, we can wake up; the story of the Buddha is not only the story of somebody long ago but it's also our own story.

Four Objects of Confidence

In Buddhism there are four objects of faith or confidence. The first is the recognition of cause and effect in our daily life. This is not just an intellectual recognition, but a deeper understanding. It is when we have those aha moments, when we understand on the visceral level that "this is because that is."

The second object of confidence is the understanding of the basic teachings of the nature of reality, such as conditioned co-arising, emptiness, or interbeing. When we're able to touch those teachings and experience them— let's say, for example, that during eating meditation you have the experience of seeing deeply that this piece of food contains the whole cosmos, that it does not exist by itself alone, there is not one condition that is lacking—then this is what is meant by touching the nature of reality and that is the second quality of confidence or faith, *shraddha*, in Buddhism.

The third object of confidence is the experience of the lived reality of the Three Refuges: the Buddha, the Dharma, and the Sangha. We experience them as lived realities in our daily life, not just as ideas. We experience the qualities of spaciousness, of an open heart, of wisdom that we call Awakening; we experience the Dharma as we go through our day. We experience our connection with the community of practice, those who have gone before and those who are going with us.

The fourth object of our faith is confidence in the effectiveness of our own Dharma practice, that we recognize and see the transformations that we have experienced and the transformations we see in others. Again, this is referring back to rejoicing in the good qualities of ourselves and others. For many of us, recognizing and having confidence in our own practice and transformation is the most challenging of the four objects.

2. Diligence

The second of the five faculties or capacities is the faculty of diligence, which is sometimes described as vigor. This means actually putting into practice the teachings that we've received. It means choosing to walk through some or one of the Dharma doors. It's nice to learn them intellectually, but we have to actually put them into practice if we want to experience a transformation. If we go to a restaurant and only read items off the menu, we're never going to satisfy our hunger and feel full unless we actually order something from the menu and we eat it.

Selective Watering

Traditionally the practice of diligence is framed in terms of the Four Right Efforts.

1. The first is consciously watering not-yet-arisen wholesome mental formations, consciously putting ourselves in situations and with people that water good qualities within us.

2. The second is maintaining already-arisen wholesome mental formations.

3. The third is selective watering: choosing not to water not-yet-arisen unwholesome mental formations.

4. The fourth is embracing and looking deeply into already-arisen unwholesome mental formations.

They're very technical terms, aren't they! Basically the Four Right Efforts support us in consciously choosing to water the wonderful qualities within ourselves and within others; putting ourselves in situations where we water those good qualities within ourselves; and, in the beginning stages of our practice, not putting ourselves in situations that water unwholesome mental formations in ourselves or in others, by which we could easily get swept away.

If an unhelpful mental formation arises, we do our very best to take good care of it so that we have the opportunity to understand it more deeply; when it sinks back down into our store consciousness, our unconscious mind, something will have changed. Do you remember earlier when we were exploring appropriate attention (yoniso manaskara)? This is an important application of appropriate attention: directing our attention in a way that is in alignment with our aspiration. In moments when an unhelpful emotion or mental formation arises, what do you find yourself dwelling on? How can you use the energy of these mental formations to bring about understanding?

3. Mindfulness

The third of the five faculties is our old friend mindfulness. We read in the beginning of the Sutra of the Four Establishments of Mindfulness, the Satipatthana Sutta, which we discussed in the previous chapter, the following phrase, "The four foundations of mindfulness are the one and only way that leads to the transcending of sorrow and sadness, to the transformation of pain and sadness, to entrance upon the right method and the realization of liberation." The one and only way: *ekayanamagga*.

The way, the path. That's a big word, a big concept, isn't it? When we speak of the Path in Buddhism, we're not speaking of a ten-lane freeway (that's easy to find, and getting even easier with tools such as GPS). But *magga* in the Pali language is associated with an ancient, overgrown hunter's path in the forest, a path that is barely discernible to the naked eye, which we really need to use all of our discernment and our sharp eyes to be able to find for ourselves.

The path is not something that is external: it exists within each one of us. What faint traces of the liberation path can you recognize in your own being as you read these words? Have you ever experienced a moment of happiness? A moment of ease, a moment of connection? Have you ever understood, even for a split second, your own self-created patterns of suffering? If so, celebrate that fact since if you look a little more closely, you will see the path underneath your feet, right here and right now.

We discover the path within us through the practice of the Four Establishments of Mindfulness: body in the body; feelings in the feelings; mental formations in mental formations; and objects of mind in objects of mind.

By the way, how are you doing in your practice of the Four Establishments of Mindfulness that we were introduced to in the previous chapter? Which ones have you found easy and which ones have you found more challenging? Did you find it easy to be with your body? Did you find it easier to be with your feelings? I invite you to continue with this practice. This is a practice that we continue the whole of our life; it's not a practice just for a few days.

4. Concentration

The fourth of the five faculties is concentration, a dwelling with the object of our attention, non-separateness from the object of our attention, whether it be our breath, body, emotions, the food we are eating, or another person. Did you know that concentration can actually be wholesome or unwholesome? If you are intent on causing damage to someone, or yourself, whether physical damage or otherwise, then that's a certain kind of concentration, isn't it? And we would not necessarily consider it wholesome. This reminds us of the importance of nurturing appropriate attention when we're developing our mindfulness, so that as we move into concentration, as our mindfulness deepens, our concentration is something that is really wholesome and in alignment with our aspiration.

5. Wisdom

The last of the five faculties is wisdom, prajña. A wise person is described in the Samyutta Nikaya as "one who knows and sees what really is," someone who does not get caught up in the conventional designation of something, someone who's able to see the larger picture. In the Visuddhimagga, the meditation text by Buddhaghosa, it is written, "Wisdom penetrates into dharmas (all things) as they are in themselves." So, wisdom penetrates into all things and sees them just as they are, in themselves.

Quantum science tells us that there is no such thing as being a passive observer. We are always participants in creation.

Wisdom, here, is not something that falls from the sky; it's not something that comes from somewhere or someone else; it is within you. Stop right here and contemplate that for a moment. Own it: wisdom exists within me and always has.

When I was a young novice, I went through a period of intense suffering. It's a long story, and it will probably be a good topic for another book. At the time, Thay said, "Brother Phap Hai, I'm always here if you need anything." A few days later, I went and knocked on Thay's door and he invited me in. As we sat drinking tea together, I shared my problem. After I finished, Thay sat quietly for a while and looked out the window. Then he turned to me and said, "Why did you come here and waste my time when you already knew what you need to do? Go and do it."

I was so angry with Thay. I guess I thought that he had blown me off. I guess I'm a pretty slow person. It wasn't until much later that I realized what a profound teaching Thay had given me. Rather than creating a situation in which I was searching for answers outside myself, he turned my attention around so I recognized that, indeed, I did know what I needed to do, I did know how to transform my situation, but I was trying to find an easier way out.

A good teacher, a good practice is one that helps you to awaken your own wisdom, your own inner teacher.

No, wisdom doesn't fall from the sky, and it's often not flashy; it might be as simple as finally recognizing and realizing a long-held destructive pattern. Venerable Pema Chödrön teaches that we might compare ourselves to a moth recognizing the pattern that it has of being inexorably drawn to the fire. Flying through the candle flame is not going to end well. It never has, and yet we're drawn to that which will destroy us until we finally recognize that pattern and turn it around. When wisdom arises, there's no effort involved in transformation.

We know what we need to do and we know what we don't need to do. What are some of the candle flames in your own life, in your own mind?

Reading

Happiness in the Present Moment

The past has already gone,
and the future has not yet come.
Let us not drown ourselves
in regret for what has passed
or in expectations and worry for the future.

The Buddha has said that we can
be peaceful, happy, and free
in this present moment.
Let us hear the Buddha's words
and let go of our sadness and anxiety.

Let us come back to ourselves
and establish ourselves in what is present right now.
Let us learn to recognize
the conditions for happiness
that are present within us
and around us.

Can we hear the birds singing
and the wind in the pines?
Can we see the green mountains,
the white clouds, the golden moon?
The Pure Land is available
in the present moment.

Every day we can enjoy ourselves
in the Buddha Land.
Every mindful breath and step
takes us to the Pure Land,

revealing all the wonders
of the Dharma body.

I am determined to let go of
hurrying, competing,
being busy and disgruntled.
I shall not run after fame, power,
riches, and sex
because I know
that this does not lead to true happiness.
All it will bring me is
misery and misfortune.

I shall learn to know what is sufficient,
to live simply,
so that I have time to live deeply
every moment of my daily life,
giving my body and mind a chance to heal,
and to have the time to look after and protect
those I have vowed to love.
I shall practice for my mind to grow
in love and compassion,
so that I have the ability to help
beings anywhere
who are drowning in craving.

I ask the Buddhas everywhere

to protect and guide me,

to support me on my path,

so that I can live in peace, joy,

and freedom every day,

fulfilling the deepest aspiration

as your disciple

whom you trust and love.

Reading

Praising the Buddha

The Buddha is like the fresh, full moon

that soars across the immense sky.

When the river of mind is truly calm,

the moon is reflected perfectly

upon the surface of the deep waters.

The countenance of the World-Honored One,

like the full moon or like the orb of the sun,

shines with the light of clarity,

a halo of wisdom spreading in every direction,

enveloping all with love, compassion, joy, and equanimity.

The inexhaustible virtues of the World-Honored One

cannot be adequately praised.

May the path of the Awakening grow brighter.

May the Dharma become clearer.

May wind and rain be favorable.

May this country be at peace in the cities and rural areas.

May all follow the way of right practice.

May nature be safe. May people in society be free and equal.

May the refreshing breeze of compassion enter into this world of heat,

allowing the sun of wisdom to shine clearly in the cloudy sky

so that the path of liberation is appreciated everywhere

and the Dharma rain falls, benefiting all species.

May the Sangha that is present here practice diligently,

showing concern and love for each other

as they would for their own family,

transforming their consciousness.

We aspire to follow the example

of the Bodhisattvas Samantabhadra and Avalokiteshvara

and all other Bodhisattva Mahasattvas,

and the Great Perfection of Wisdom.[*]

---

[*] Thich Nhat Hanh, *Chanting from the Heart*.

Questions for Reflection

1. As I become more grounded in body and mind, what "hindrances" am I aware of most strongly through my day? Are there some that are more predominant?

2. What does *waking up* mean to me? What are some of the candle flames of my own life, my own heart?

Six Ways to Cross Over to the Other Shore

There is a beautiful Zen story about the awakening of Mahakashyapa, who was one of the great disciples of the Buddha. One day, everyone had gathered to hear the Buddha give a teaching. The Buddha, seeing that Mahakashyapa was ready for enlightenment, silently held up a single flower; that's all he did. I can imagine that there were some in the crowd who wondered what was going on—they had gathered to hear a Dharma talk! Perhaps they felt cheated or confused, and were thinking impatiently, "When are we going to receive a Dharma talk?"

Mahakashyapa in that moment looked up and was able to see the flower as it truly was. In that moment the Buddha transmitted the mind, the essence of the Dharma to Mahakashyapa.

The Buddha actively taught for about forty-five years and offered so many teachings over the years of his ministry.

He offered guidance that was appropriate to the need and to the occasion and tailored to the audience that was there. When I read the sutras, I see that the Buddha was a very, very skillful teacher. What was necessary to teach about in one situation was not always appropriate in another, or to another person with different tendencies and a different mindset. This is one aspect of a quality called *upaya* or skillful means: teachings that are appropriate to the time, the person, and the occasion.

Mahakashyapa had heard most of the oral teachings of the Buddha, and yet in that moment he was ready for another kind of understanding to emerge.

Did the Buddha transmit something to Mahakashyapa, or did he awaken something that was already there? When we consider the story of Mahakashyapa, one question I often ask myself is, What kind of flower is being held up to me in this moment? What kinds of flowers are being held up for me in each moment of my daily life?

The Shore of Liberation

The framework we've been using thus far in this book is the framework of Dharma Doors; this is one poetic image that elucidates and explains the Buddhadharma. Another metaphor that's commonly used is the image of crossing a river to the other shore. There's a shore of suffering, a shore that we call the saha world: a world of red dust, of pairs of opposites where there's birth, there's death, there's suffering, there's happiness. Integral to the idea of a shore of suffering is another shore, which is called the shore of liberation. Using this imagery, the teachings are described as a raft that we use to cross the raging torrent to reach the other shore. Once we reach the other shore, then we no longer need the raft in its current form.

When I reflect on this imagery, a couple of things come to my mind. Firstly, each one of us is a little bit different. Some of us have a lot of luggage when we begin our journey to the other shore. If you don't believe this, just go to the airport and have a look around. Others of us begin the journey with little. In this simple example, each of the passengers would need a very different kind of raft, built of different kinds of planks of Dharma teachings.

Looking at your situation at this point in time, at this moment in your journey, what kind of Dharma teachings and practices are the planks that you need to pick up and use to create a raft to cross the raging torrent of suffering?

The second thing that comes to my mind when I think about this metaphor of crossing the torrent is that once we get to the other shore we're advised to let go of the raft, because we no longer need it. But the question that comes to my mind is: Does that mean that the raft has only one function and that once we're on the other shore it's of no more use?

It occurs to me that perhaps when we get to the other shore, we're going to discover other uses for the raft. The raft of the Dharma, to me, is not a means to an end, it's the end itself. Our practice of meditation is not a means to an end—it is the end itself. There is no way home: home is the way.

We live in a world of duality, and even in the above metaphor, there is the duality of a "shore of suffering" that needs to be left behind in order to reach the "shore of liberation."

The Two Truths Inter-Are

In Chapter two we spoke about the Two Truths: the historical dimension and the ultimate dimension. In the historical dimension we're in a pair of opposites: there's this and that; there's me and you; there's before and after; there's the shore of suffering, the *saha* world that must be endured, the red dust of dissatisfaction, of pain, of separation, and there's a journey to be made, a crossing of the river, a raging torrent.

In the ultimate dimension, looking with the eyes of ultimate truth, the path, the journey is liberation itself. We cross the water only to realize that the two banks of the river are one, that the journey that appeared to be from one place to another—the shore of suffering to the shore of liberation—was less of a journey than a shifting of perception to discover where we have been all along.

By the way, the journey from one shore to another is not a one-time event. It is a journey that we are making constantly with different aspects of our being.

It is important to understand that the historical and ultimate realities are not in opposition to each other. They're not another pair of opposites. This would be our natural tendency to think in this way, particularly as we're conditioned to think in a binary sense. But in the Buddhist world, the Two Truths inter-are and they depend on each other.

It might come down to our way of seeing things. In the texts, an interesting example is mentioned. If we place a glass of water on the table, something that we do at least a couple of times a day, a human being will see it as a glass of water; a hungry ghost, which in the Buddhist world is a being who is deeply isolated and feeling cut off from all love and connectedness, will see that glass of water as a cup of poison or raging fire; and a divine being will see it as *amrita*, as nectar. So who is seeing the water just as it is? Are we simply an observer, or do we participate in the creation of our experience?

I often use a simple example when I'm giving a teaching, of all of us sitting together in the same room sharing the same space and the same conditions—the warmth, the cushions that we're sitting on, the chair. So in the physical sense we're all in the same place. At the same time, we're all in very different realms. Some of us are feeling too warm, some of us are too cold, some of us are totally blissed out, and some of us are completely bored. Who's right and who's wrong and what's the objective reality here? That which we so easily call "reality" is always interpretation, and it depends on our way of seeing things.

By the way, I hope you haven't gotten this far into this little book and discovered that I bore you, but if you have, I'm excited at the opportunity that this presents for you!

Bodhicitta

In the Plum Village tradition we practice Mahayana Buddhism, the "Great Vehicle." Mahayana Buddhism is sometimes described as *paramitayana*, the vehicle of crossing over, or the vehicle of cultivating the perfections. Our journey within the Great Vehicle really begins when we touch and begin to cultivate a very precious seed that we all have within us. That seed is called *bodhicitta*; Thay calls bodhicitta "the mind of love."

Love here is not a small, limited love, but a deep

cherishing of ourself and of all living beings, which gives rise to a wish to be of benefit. When we look deeply at our own situation and all of the dissatisfaction and difficulties we face, and we look deeply at the situation of others, if we're a person who's able to recognize the many kindnesses that are being offered to us in every moment, then very naturally a beautiful quality of mind begins to emerge called bodhicitta, the wish that we be of benefit for all beings who are not separate from ourselves.

Everything, all the good conditions we enjoy right now in this moment, haven't come about through our own efforts alone, but through the efforts of so many living beings—beings who have created the roads, who've built the buildings, who've offered us employment, who've created the food that we enjoy. So many good conditions have come to us thanks to the kindness of others. One of the great barriers in our heart to cultivating this beautiful seed of bodhicitta is our sense of entitlement. "I deserve all of these things—they've all come about thanks to my own efforts. All of you are just lazy and haven't really contributed anything."

Recognizing the great web of kindness that we exist in and we benefit from is the first step of the emergence of bodhicitta. This mind of love, bodhicitta, is the very essence of the Great Vehicle path. I'm not a separate self, a lonely, isolated individual separated from others. But I'm deeply connected in this web of kindness. So much has been done and is being done to make my life possible and beautiful.

This fundamental interconnectedness of all things is referred to in Buddhism as emptiness, or interbeing. Emptiness here is not a nihilistic rejection of existence, but rather a deep recognition of the interconnectedness of all phenomena.

Intention and Action

There's a wonderful text by Shantideva called "The Way of the Bodhisattva" (Bodhicariyavatara), and in that text, bodhicitta, the mind of love, is described as a flash of lightning that illuminates all that's there. Bodhicitta helps us to see things clearly, to see things in a wider sense than we normally experience them; like a flash of lightning, the mind of love illuminates the world "outside" and the world "inside."

Bodhicitta is described as having two aspects: *bodhicitta as intention*, and *bodhicitta as action*.

Bodhicitta as intention is the wish to benefit ourselves and others; it's like an aspiration. Perhaps we could describe it as an intention to go on a journey.

Bodhicitta as action is actually setting out on the journey that we envisage, actually opening the door and taking steps on the path in the direction that we envisage.

Just between you and me, I think that many of us are exceptionally good at the first aspect of bodhicitta: *bodhicitta as intention*, but we experience greater challenges with transforming intention into action. Why do you think that is?

Isolation and Connection

To return to the image we used earlier of building a raft to cross over to the other shore, the Pali canon describes six practices, six ways of "crossing over" called the *paramitas*: generosity, the precepts, inclusiveness, energy, meditation, and insight. These are the pieces of wood with which we can build our vessel.

As I reflect on these six crossings-over, I'm struck again and again by the fact that they all help us to reach out of our isolation and connect with others. This is perhaps the biggest crossing-over of our time, the big delusion that we suffer that we're somehow separate, that we're isolated individuals without a connection to others and the world around us. We have never, in the recorded history of humankind, been more connected through technological means, but we still feel isolated and alone.

These Six Paramitas are the very journey itself; they're the timbers of our raft and our way to cross the stream of suffering. They are bodhicitta as intention, in terms of generating aspiration; and they're also bodhicitta as action, because they are practices to apply in our daily life.

The Four Qualities

In Mahayana Buddhism, those who have generated this seed of bodhicitta, the mind of love, and are practicing the crossings-over of the paramitas are called bodhisattvas. A bodhisattva is also someone who has made the great vow. This is not a vow to win the lotto or to go to Hawaii, but a great vow, a vow to be of benefit to living beings, wherever we may find ourselves.

Traditionally in Mahayana Buddhism there are four great archetypal bodhisattvas that refer to four great qualities that we want to cultivate in our own practice of awakening and manifesting bodhicitta as intention and bodhicitta in action.

1. Great Understanding

The first of these bodhisattvas is Manjushri, the Bodhisattva of Great Understanding, who wields a sword of wisdom to cut through delusion. This is the quality of discernment. The sword of Manjushri refers to a concentrated mind, a one-pointed mind that doesn't get caught up in all kinds of surface appearances and distractions. We know what we're doing, why we're doing it, and who we're doing it with.

2. Great Action

The second of the four great archetypal bodhisattvas in the Mahayana tradition is Samantabhadra. This is the Bodhisattva of Great Action—manifesting wisdom through action. The energy of Samantabhadra helps us to move from the realm of wisdom as intention into wisdom as daily action. We begin to release the idea that we might do such and such a thing later when conditions are miraculously favorable, and begin to realize that this moment is the perfect moment to open our heart.

I remember in high school, one of my classmates was nicknamed "Gunna." *Gunna* is the Australian slang way of saying "going to." Whenever we would offer him some advice, he would reply, "Yeah, I'm gunna do that one of these days." And honestly, in my heart of hearts, I think for most of us as practitioners, our nickname is also Gunna. We're gunna do this, we're gunna do that, we're gunna do what is beneficial—but only when the conditions are "right." We have a raincheck mentality: when all the conditions are perfect we'll get around to it and we'll do it, or we'll say the words that have been hidden in our hearts all of these years. This is the beauty of cultivating the capacity of great action within us. We actually bring our bodhicitta, our intentions, into action.

3. Great Compassion

The third great bodhisattva is Avalokiteshvara, the Bodhisattva of Great Compassion, the Bodhisattva of Deep Listening. *Avalokiteshvara* actually means "She Who Hears the Cries of the World"—the cries of all sentient beings in the world "out there" and also the cries of the world within: the world within our own mind, within our own heart. The cries of the world out there are not separate from the cries within our own being, within our own heart. Developing the capacity to be present with what's there, to hear what's being shared, and also what's not yet able to be shared. I often share with my friends that to learn to meditate is to learn how to listen with all of our being; to be completely open and listen with our ears first of all, then learning to listen with our eyes, with our mind, with our whole being.

4. Great Determination

The fourth great bodhisattva is Kshitigarbha, the Earth Store Bodhisattva, the Bodhisattva of the Great Vow. Kshitigarbha is sometimes described as the greatest of all the bodhisattvas because he or she made the vow to enter hell, to enter the darkest places, the places of despair, and to be present with beings that are suffering greatly. He or she made the vow that they will always remain in the darkest places until all beings are rescued. This paradoxical vow, "living beings are limitless, I vow to rescue them, I vow to be present, with them all," is the vow of the Bodhisattva of Great Aspiration. The fourth quality here is the quality of determination, of non-fear, directed toward our own suffering and the suffering of others.

I find it very interesting that in iconography, Kshitigarbha is often depicted as holding a wish-fulfilling jewel in his hand, a jewel that's incredibly radiant and that illuminates the darkest places. In the text that I mentioned earlier, "The Way of the Bodhisattva," bodhicitta itself is described as being a wish-fulfilling jewel, a jewel that helps us to manifest peace, to manifest stability, to manifest compassion for ourselves and for those around us.

Right understanding, beneficial action, great compassion, and the deep aspiration to be present for living beings, these are the fundamental mind qualities of the Mahayana path. They are the qualities of bodhicitta in intention, as well as also being the manifestation of bodhicitta in action. We might wonder, "What does bodhicitta look like?" These four qualities—of understanding; of acting to benefit self and others; of generating and offering compassion to myself and to others; as well as the aspiration, the deep vow, to always be there by the side of those in need—are bodhicitta in action.

The Six Paramitas

The Six that we often refer to in Mahayana Buddhism are the Six Paramitas, the six crossings-over.

1. Generosity

The first crossing-over is generosity. We have already explored together the three kinds of generosity: material gifts (food, money, books, clothing); gifts of Dharma, which don't need to be anything extraordinary (one example might be a well-chosen word that helps someone to awaken a beautiful quality in her heart; another could be a smile, or the sound of a bell); and the gift of non-fear.

2. Precepts

The second of the paramitas is the practice of precepts, which act as mindfulness trainings. Many of us in the Buddhist tradition have received at least Five Precepts; monks take more mindfulness trainings than laypeople, and within the monastic community the number often increases with seniority. There are the Five Precepts, the Fourteen, the Two Hundred and Fifty, the Three Hundred and Forty-Eight, and so on. Often people ask, "Why are there so many different precepts?" At their core, the mindfulness trainings, regardless of the number, are all elucidations of what we call the Three Cumulative Pure Precepts. That's a bit of a mouthful, isn't it? These Three Precepts, and indeed all the precepts, can be summed up in the following three phrases:

* The first Pure Precept is "refraining from harmful actions of body, speech, and mind." Refraining from actions that harm myself or others, whether by thought, action, or speech.

* The second is "cultivating wholesome seeds in self and others." Cultivating the qualities of understanding, love, compassion, and joy within ourselves and nurturing those seeds in others. When we see a talent or a capacity in somebody else, we take every opportunity to nurture that capacity, to water that good quality. The capacities that other people have may not be the same capacities that we have. So we nurture what is beneficial and what's wholesome in the other person as well as what's beneficial and wholesome in ourselves.

* The third of the Cumulative Pure Precepts is "to benefit all beings," to live in a way that we bring joy, we bring happiness, to those we interact with. Thay shares this practice as "offering joy to one person in the morning and helping relieve the suffering of one person in the afternoon."

3. Inclusiveness

The third of the paramitas is usually referred to as patience. In the Plum Village tradition, we like to refer to it as inclusiveness. This quality is not a sense of forbearance, of putting up with or tolerating unwanted things, but rather a spaciousness and an openness of heart. It's about not leaving anyone or anything out.

There's a funny story in the Chinese tradition that I like a lot. I first heard it about twenty years ago, and it brings a little chuckle to me every time I think about it. Here is my retelling of the tale.

The Hermit Who Practiced Patience

There was a hermit living in a cave, quite a number of years ago, outside of a small village in China. He had a sign in front of his cave that read, "Supreme Master of Patience." As you would expect, his cave became a major pilgrimage site, and the local villagers were so glad and proud to have this master nearby who was the perfection of patience. The master got a little proud one day, and made another sign: "My nature is the nature of ashes." What he meant by that enigmatic phrase is that all the roots of greed, hatred, and delusion had been completely eradicated within him, and that he was the manifestation of perfect patience.

From near and far away they came to visit him. As the months and years went by, his fame grew such that the village idiot decided to go on a pilgrimage to visit him as well. When he arrived, he pushed his way through the milling crowd and saw the two signs. Not being able to read, he shouted out to the hermit: "Hey you, what does that say?"

The hermit looked upon him kindly and replied, "My nature is the nature of ashes."

The village idiot thought for a moment and said, "But what does it *mean*?" The hermit responded, "It means that I, my friend, have perfected patience." The village idiot asked, "What's patience?" The hermit answered, "Patience is the capacity to be present with everyone, no matter what their circumstances." The village idiot said, "Come again?"

And the hermit said, "I am a Perfect Patient One." The village idiot said, "I just don't get it." So the hermit tried to help him by saying, "I am practicing the perfection of patience." The village idiot looked at him out of the corner of his eye and asked, "What's patience again?"

This questioning went on from the early morning until late afternoon. The village idiot would ask a question and the hermit would respond, but the village idiot would not understand and the questioning would continue.

Very late in the afternoon, the village idiot said, "I just can't understand, no matter how many times you answer the question. I don't understand what you're practicing." At this, the hermit finally stood up and said, "Damn you! Damn you! No matter how many times I explain it you just won't understand. Why have you even bothered to come here and waste my precious time like this?"

The village idiot smiled, stood up, and said, "You have not even begun to practice or understand the perfection of patience," and then walked away back to the town. The hermit then left the cave and went off to practice in a faraway place.

When I think of this story, I think I probably wouldn't last as long as the hermit, I think I'd be done in about an hour or so. I still admire the hermit a little bit for being able to hold out all those many hours with the questions.

We all need our village idiots. They are actually bodhisattvas in disguise. A village idiot might not necessarily be a person; it might be a situation in which all our facades, all of our masks, the things we hide behind come crumbling down, and we see our true situation. Hooray for village idiots, celebrate them, welcome them, invite them in, because they are powerful spurs to growth. What are some of the village idiot moments in your life?

Coming back to the paramita of patience, it's important that our mindset is not, "I am patient with some condition or someone that's outside of myself." This is why I love Thay's retranslation of the word *kshanti* as inclusiveness. Inclusiveness means that we don't see ourselves and the other person, or this condition, as separate, but that we are interconnected.

4. Energy

The next of the paramitas is energy or diligence, which we explored together as the Four Right Efforts. Never forget, when exploring the paramita of energy, of diligence, the element of taking delight in the practice. You look forward to it and the joy of meditation becomes your daily food.

5. Meditation

The fifth of the paramitas is meditation or *dhyana*. Dhyana actually means absorption, or another way to describe it is one-pointedness. This is not a neurotic one-pointedness where we shut everything out and we're closed down, but a quality of mind that embraces all and excludes none, a quality of seeing all and embracing all: both sides of the equation, nothing's excluded. And "nothing excluded" here is not only in terms of conditions in our heart, but also in terms of the activities of our daily life—that our meditation is not only confined to the cushion, but our meditation is our daily life. So when we're talking about one-pointedness, of embracing all, we're also talking about bringing this spacious awareness to everything that we're doing. This is a perfection for us to practice, this is one "crossing over" that can help us to be able to cross over the shore of our separateness.

6. Insight

And the sixth of the crossings-over is insight, prajña, seeing things as they really are. *Prajñaparamita* is described as the mother of all the buddhas. Giving birth to insight within us is giving birth to the buddha that is within us: our awakened understanding. I find it interesting that the Buddha's mother's name is recorded in the sutras as being "Mahamaya," which means Great Illusion. What is the great illusion? The great illusion is that the Buddha is only someone who lived thousands of years ago. We know that in the Prajñaparamita literature, insight is described as being the mother of all buddhas. By developing wisdom, our practice is to give birth to the Buddha in the sense of giving birth to the Awakened Mind.

The Paramitas Inter-Are

Thay describes the paramitas as petals of a flower; they're all connected to each other. In practicing one, we're practicing them all in the sense that as we cultivate one, the others develop at the same time. All of these Six Paramitas are already present within our mind to a greater or lesser extent. When we generate bodhicitta and we start walking on the Mahayana path, then we can choose to cultivate these qualities that are naturally present in our mind. We can choose to make them the framework of our raft.

Let's consider how the paramitas develop in tandem. This is very good news for a lazy person such as myself—that by cultivating one we cultivate them all! Let's choose one at random; let's say mindfulness trainings. Is there an element of generosity in my practice of the mindfulness trainings? How is my practice of the mindfulness trainings a practice of giving, a practice of generosity? What am I giving to myself and to others when I practice the mindfulness trainings? How has my practice of the mindfulness trainings helped me to develop inclusiveness, patience, and a robust sense of humor? I think that's another aspect of inclusiveness—a robust sense of humor—because we don't, we can't, take ourselves too seriously anymore. We're able to see our mind as it really works. So how does my practice of the mindfulness trainings help me to develop inclusiveness and a sense of humor?

What's my experience of energy, of having more energy and more diligence through the practice of the mindfulness trainings? How do the mindfulness trainings inform my meditation, my one-pointedness? Do they? What insights have I developed thanks to the practice of the mindfulness trainings?

There's a teaching about the mindfulness trainings that says when you receive the mindfulness trainings, you're receiving the very body of the Awakened One. In the traditional texts, taking the trainings is referred to as receiving a prediction of enlightenment. If you practice the mindfulness trainings, for sure you're going to wake up. In the monastic ordination ceremony when we become a novice, our teacher comes and places his hand on our head, and it's just like how the traditional text describes the Buddha coming and placing his hand on your head and predicting that you will become a buddha. When we take the mindfulness trainings, regardless of the number, it's like the Awakened One coming and saying, "For sure you're going to awaken; there are no two ways about it!"

This contemplation can be done for all the paramitas, seeing how they all arise in tandem with each other. It can be a wonderful contemplation for us to do.

Consider contemplating your practice through the framework of the paramitas this week: In generating one quality we're generating them all. The paramitas are like precious jewels that we've been holding in our palm all along.

Reading

Sutra on the Eight Realizations of the Great Beings

Wholeheartedly, day and night, disciples of the Awakened One should recite and meditate on the Eight Realizations discovered by the Great Beings.

The First Realization is the awareness that the world is impermanent. Political regimes are subject to fall. Things composed of the four elements are empty, containing within them the seeds of suffering. Human beings are composed of Five Aggregates and are without a separate self. They are always in the process of change—constantly being born and constantly dying. They are empty of self and without a separate existence. The mind is the source of all confusion, and the body the forest of all unwholesome actions.

Meditating on this, you can be released from the round of birth and death.

The Second Realization is the awareness that more desire brings more suffering. All hardships in daily life arise from greed and desire. Those with little desire and ambition are able to relax, their body and mind free from entanglement.

The Third Realization is the awareness that the human mind is always searching outside itself and never feels fulfilled. This brings about unwholesome activity. Bodhisattvas, on the other hand, know the value of having few desires. They live simply and peacefully, so they can devote themselves to practicing the Way. They regard the realization of perfect understanding to be their only career.

The Fourth Realization is the awareness that indolence is an obstacle to practice. You must practice diligently to transform unwholesome mental states that bind you, and you must conquer the four kinds of Mara in order to free yourself from the prisons of the Five Aggregates and the Three Worlds.

The Fifth Realization is the awareness that ignorance is the cause of the endless round of birth and death. Bodhisattvas always listen to and learn from others so their understanding and skillful means can develop, and so they can teach living beings and bring them great joy.

The Sixth Realization is the awareness that poverty creates hatred and anger, which creates a vicious cycle of negative thoughts and actions. When practicing generosity, bodhisattvas consider everyone—friends and enemies alike—to be equal. They do not condemn anyone's past wrongdoings or hate even those presently causing harm.

The Seventh Realization is the awareness that the five categories of sensual desire—money, sex, fame, overeating, and oversleeping—lead to problems. Although you are in the world, try not to be caught in worldly matters. A monastic, for example, has in their possession only three robes and one bowl. They live simply in order to practice the Way. Their precepts keep them free of entanglement with worldly things, and they treat everyone equally and with compassion.

The Eighth Realization is the awareness that the fire of birth and death is raging, causing endless suffering everywhere. Take the Great Vow to help all beings, to suffer with all beings, and to guide all beings to the Realm of Great Joy.

These Eight Realizations are the discoveries of great beings, buddhas and bodhisattvas who have practiced diligently the way of understanding and love. They have sailed the Dharmakaya boat to the shore of nirvana, and have then returned to the ordinary world, free of the five sensual desires, their minds and hearts directed toward the Noble Way. Using these Eight Realizations, they help all beings recognize the suffering in the world.

If disciples of the Buddha recite and meditate on these Eight Realizations, they will put an end to countless misunderstandings and difficulties and progress toward enlightenment, leaving behind the world of birth and death, dwelling forever in peace.*

---

* Taisho Revised Tripitaka 779. See Thich Nhat Hanh, *Chanting from the Heart*.

Reading
Universal Door Chapter of the Lotus Sutra

Introductory Gatha

Chanting the Lotus Sutra by night,

the sound shook the galaxies.

The next morning when planet Earth woke up,

her lap was full of flowers.

Discourse

Buddha of ten thousand beautiful aspects,

may I ask you this question:

"Why did they give that bodhisattva

the name Avalokita?"

The World-Honored One, beautifully adorned,

offered this reply to Akshayamati:

"Because actions founded on her deep aspiration

can respond to the needs of any being in any circumstance.

"Aspirations as wide as the oceans

were made for countless lifetimes.

She has attended to billions of Buddhas,

her great aspiration purified by mindfulness.

"Whoever calls her name or sees her image,

if their mind be perfectly collected and pure,

they will then be able to overcome

the suffering of all the worlds.

"When those with cruel intent

push us into a pit of fire,

invoking the strength of Avalokita,

the fire becomes a refreshing lake.

"Adrift on the waters of the great ocean,

threatened by monsters of the deep,

invoking the strength of Avalokita,

we are saved from the storm waves.

"Standing atop Mount Meru,

should someone desire to push us down,

invoking the strength of Avalokita,

we dwell unharmed like the sun hanging in space.

"Chased by a cruel person

down the Diamond Mountain,

invoking the strength of Avalokita,

not even a hair of our body will be in danger.

"Encircled and assaulted by bandits

holding swords to wound and to kill,

invoking the strength of Avalokita,

sword blades shatter into millions of pieces.

"Imprisoned or bound in iron chains,

with hands and feet placed in a yoke,

invoking the strength of Avalokita,

we are released into freedom.

"Poisons, curses, and bewitchings

putting us into danger,

invoking the strength of Avalokita,

harmful things return to their source.

"Attacked by a fierce and cruel yaksha,

a poisonous naga, or unkind spirit,

invoking the strength of Avalokita,

they will do us no harm.

"With wild animals all around

baring their teeth, tusks, and claws,

invoking the strength of Avalokita

will cause them to run far away.

"Confronted with scorpions and poisonous snakes,

breathing fire and smoke of poisonous gas,

invoking the strength of Avalokita,

they depart, the air clears.

"Caught beneath lightning, thunder, and clouds,

with hail pouring down in torrents,

invoking the strength of Avalokita,

the storm ends, the sunlight appears.

"All living beings caught in distress,

oppressed by immeasurable suffering

are rescued in ten thousand ways

by the wonderful power of her understanding.

"Miraculous power with no shortcoming,

wisdom and skillful means so vast—

in the Ten Directions of all the worlds,

there is no place she does not appear.

"The paths to realms of suffering,

the pain of birth, old age, sickness, and death,

hells, hungry spirits, or animals

are all purified, brought to an end.

"Look of truth, look of purity,

look of boundless understanding,

look of love, look of compassion—

the look to be always honored and practiced.

"Look of immaculate light and purity,

the Sun of Wisdom destroying darkness,

master of fire, wind, and disaster

illuminating the whole world.

"Heart of compassion like rolling thunder,

heart of love like gentle clouds,

water of Dharma nectar raining upon us,

extinguishing the fire of afflictions.

"In the courtroom, the place of lawsuits,

on the fields in the midst of war,

invoking the strength of Avalokita,

our enemies become our friends.

"Sound of wonder, noble sound,

sound of one looking deeply into the world,

extraordinary sound, sound of the rising tide,

the sound to which we will always listen.

"With mindfulness, free from doubts,

in moments of danger and affliction,

our faith in the purity of Avalokita

is where we go for refuge.

"We bow in gratitude to the one

who has all the virtues,

regarding the world with compassionate eyes,

an Ocean of Well-Being beyond measure."[*]

Questions for Reflection

1. Do I notice any "flower" moments this week? What are some situations where I am called to a deeper understanding, a widening of my heart?

2. Reflecting on the paramitas—which one(s) are most present for me in my practice and daily life at this time?

3. Take some time to reflect concretely on the interconnectedness of the paramitas and how they manifest themselves in your practice, for example, how is generosity a part of the mindfulness trainings, how is inclusiveness part of the trainings et cetera, until you have

---

[*] Saddharmapundarika Sutra, Chapter 25, Taisho Revised Tripitaka 262. See Thich Nhat Hanh, *Chanting from the Heart.*

looked at all of them and their different manifestations? This is a really interesting reflection and you are going to discover many aspects to your practice and motivation that you hadn't touched until now! Enjoy!

4. What does compassion mean to me? How does compassion manifest in my life? How can compassion be a protection?

5. In the Discourse on the Eight Realizations of Great Beings, what does "to suffer with all beings" mean to me?

Suggested Practice
Walking Meditation

Walking meditation is a very powerful practice of moving meditation. Usually in our daily lives when we walk, we are walking to "get" somewhere. When we practice walking meditation, we are going nowhere, except to this step, this breath. There are many wonderful methods of walking meditation, many of which are outlined in the book *How to Walk.* * As a gentle beginning practice, notice the sensation of your feet on the earth and as you breathe in, take two or three steps, and as you breathe out you may like to take four or five steps, depending on the length of your in-breath and out-breath.

---

* Thich Nhat Hanh, *How to Walk* (Berkeley: Parallax Press, 2015).

Create space and time, this week for walking meditation, both a focused period of perhaps fifteen minutes a day of walking meditation and a natural practice of embodied walking as you move through your day. Notice times and spaces where you feel relaxed and unhurried, and situations in which you feel rushed and "pressed."

CHAPTER SEVEN

The Seven Factors of Awakening

I keep returning to the little book of sutras called *Some Sayings of the Buddha.*[*] There's a story that really touched me when I first read it years ago, and which opened up for me a new understanding of the kind of teacher the Buddha was. It is contained in a sutra called "The Analysis of the Properties." It is illustrative of the kind of teacher that the Buddha was.

Reading

The Story of Pukkusati Meeting the Buddha

On one occasion the Buddha was wandering from town to town in the region of Magadha in India, and he came to the town of Rajagriha. Upon entering the town he went to the

---

* F. L. Woodward, *Some Sayings of the Buddha* (New Delhi: Asian Educational Services, 2002).

house of a potter called Bhaggava.

The Buddha knocked on the door and said to him, "If it's not a problem for you, may I stay overnight in your shed?"

Bhaggava responded, "Well, it's no problem for me at all. You're more than welcome to stay in my shed. But right now there's another wanderer, another ascetic who's staying in my shed. So if it's okay with you, it would be great if you could check with him."

The Buddha said, "Certainly, I'll check and see if it's okay with him." The Buddha made his way out back to the shed and he met the ascetic in the shed who introduced himself as Pukkusati.

Pukkusati had become a monk, having left home after he came into contact with members of the Sangha and heard a teaching of the Buddha from them.

Even though he had become a monastic, he'd never actually seen or met the Buddha in person. So when the Buddha entered the shed, Pukkusati had no idea who it was.

The Buddha said, "Hello, is it possible for me to stay overnight in this shed with you?" And Pukkusati replied to him, "There's heaps of space! You're more than welcome if you would like to stay, just set yourself up in the corner over there."

The Buddha entered the shed and piled up some hay in one corner and sat down in sitting meditation. He sat for a period of time and Pukkusati did the same thing.

After their sitting meditation, the Buddha turned to Pukkusati and asked him, "So tell me a little bit about your own practice. Who are you a disciple of and what is the teaching of your teacher?"

Pukkusati replied to him, "There is, friend, Gotama the monk. He's a member of the Shakya tribe. And the excellent story about Gotama that's being spread around, is that he's worthy, he's rightly self-awakened, he's consummate in knowledge and conduct, he's well-gone, an expert with regard to the worlds, unexcelled as a trainer for people fit to be trained, the teacher of divine and human beings, he's awakened, and fully enlightened. I became a monastic out of dedication to that teacher, and it's that teacher's teaching that I follow, that I take refuge in."

And then the Buddha delightfully asks Pukkusati, "Where does this blessed one live, where is he staying right now?"

Pukkusati replied to him, "Well, there's a city in the north called Savatthi and that's where the Buddha is staying right now."

"Have you ever seen him? Or if you saw him do you think you would you recognize him?"

Pukkusati replied, "I've never seen the blessed one before and so I wouldn't recognize him if I came into contact with him."

And then the Buddha reflected for a moment: it's out of dedication to me that this person has gone forth into the spiritual life. How about I give him a teaching that will awaken his eye of Dharma? So the Buddha said to Pukkusati, "Let me offer you a teaching." And Pukkusati said, "I will listen."

And then the Buddha went on to give him a very beautiful teaching. If you want to experience it for yourself you can look up Majjhima Nikaya 140, "The Discourse on the Analysis of the Properties."

As the Buddha was speaking, Pukkusati's Dharma eye began to open and he recognized who was sitting in front of him and teaching him. As the Buddha continued to offer this very beautiful teaching to Pukkusati, Pukkusati joined his palms and bowed before the Buddha and he asked the Buddha to allow him to be fully ordained.

I'm most moved in this story by the Buddha's humility and the fact that the Buddha was so unassuming and so approachable for people, and met people where they were at, creating the right conditions for people to wake up, for their hearts to be touched, for them to be able to receive the teaching that was appropriate for them in whichever situation they found themselves in.

Waking Up

Buddhism is fundamentally about waking up—whether it's waking up to who's in front of us, or waking up to what we're doing, or waking up to what's going on in our mind. In fact, Buddhism actually means the way of waking up: how to wake up.

When I was a young boy growing up in Australia, almost every day of my life, I received what I now view as a very pithy Buddhist teaching. My parents, teachers, and many other adults used to tell me, "Hey, you'd better wake up to yourself, boy." It was only much later that I discovered the methods to put that teaching into practice!

What does waking up mean to you? What is it that you need to wake up to in this moment, in this encounter, in this situation?

The Buddha recognized that there is much suffering and dissatisfaction in our life and that, at our most fundamental level, we want to heal it, we want to understand it. This is one of the driving forces of our life; it is at our core. We don't want to suffer; we want happiness, however we view it. But we keep looking in the wrong places; we keep searching for things that can't heal our situation, that only create more pain and suffering over time. This is the trap that we're caught in.

We see and yet don't want to acknowledge the

impermanent nature of things, so we hold on to things, on to people, on to situations, on to positions, and on to ideas that we imagine are going to give us the security that we crave, that we most want. We never quite put two and two together in order to find a real and lasting place of refuge.

A Kind Spiritual Friend

When I reflect on the factors contributing to waking up, as well as my own journey, I think that for each one of us, one of the primary factors is that we've encountered a kind spiritual friend of some form or another. One time after a Dharma discussion, Ananda, the Buddha's attendant, came to the Buddha and said, "Noble friendship, it's half of the holy life." The Buddha looked at him and said, "Well, that's not true, Ananda, that's not true at all." (I can just imagine the look on Ananda's face at this point.) Then the Buddha continued, "Noble friendship, wise companionship, is the whole of the holy life."

At a certain point in our life, a kind friend spoke a word of Dharma to us, gave us a book, or brought us to a talk or to a practice center, or something of that nature, and it touched a seed, a spark in us. It awoke something in us.

It is also a nice practice to consider any supportive condition we encounter as a kind spiritual friend. Whenever I sit down on my cushion in the meditation hall, I bow, because I see that cushion as a very kind friend to my buttocks and lower back. Whenever I practice in this way, I experience a lot of joy and gratitude, because I am not taking things for granted.

Seeing the Nature of Awakening in Everyone

In the Lotus Sutra there's a bodhisattva called Never Despising; sometimes his name is translated as "Always Despised." He goes around bowing to everyone and telling them that he honors them deeply because he can see the Buddha nature in them: that they're going to become buddhas one day.

So everyone thinks, "Well, this guy's a nutcase."

Being able to recognize the essential quality of goodness in another person is actually a very beautiful practice. In the Plum Village tradition we do it when we join our palms, coming back to ourselves and looking at the other person, we bow to them and say the gatha, "A lotus for you, a Buddha to be."

Are we able to look at the members of our Sangha or our family in that way? How are the members of my Sangha or my family supportive conditions on the path? How have they been kind spiritual friends to me? What kind spiritual friends have I met on my path so far that have helped me to reach this place where I'm encountering teachings of healing, teachings of transformation?

Before we move on, I'd like to address the elephant in the room. Never Despising Bodhisattva in the Lotus Sutra didn't just congratulate and bow to the conventionally kind and wonderful people: he bowed to and congratulated *everyone*—even the most difficult. If we know how to benefit from their presence, difficult people might be the kindest spiritual friends of all.

Skillful Means

Let's return to the beautiful teaching called upaya, which translates as skillful means, to develop the capacity to respond appropriately to the need and the situation. We encountered the Buddha's upaya with the story of Mahakashyapa. We know that in the Buddha's time he used many skillful means in order to reach different people and to touch the deep longing we all have for liberation. The story of Pukkusati earlier in this chapter is another example. Another example that comes to my mind of the exquisite skillfulness of the Buddha is the famous story of Kisa Gotami.

Kisa Gotami and the Mustard Seed

Kisa Gotami had given birth to a son whom she loved dearly. One day he passed away suddenly and she was distraught. She was a disciple of the Buddha and the following thought came to her: "If anyone can help me, the Buddha can." So she carried the corpse of her son in her arms to the Buddha and laid it in front of him, saying, "Please help me, please revive my son."

The Buddha looked at her and compassionately said, "Sure, I will revive your son for you, but I need one thing in order to do it. I just need some mustard seed from a house that's never seen death. Can you get that for me?" Kisa Gotami was ecstatic and she said, "Yes, it's easy to get some mustard seed from a house that's never seen death. I'll be back soon."

So she went from house to house in the village knocking at the door and asking, "Has your house ever seen death?" At every house she went to, people had experienced the death of a loved one.

Gradually as she went through the village a couple of things occurred. She began to be able to accept the fact of death, and came to understand that it is something we all experience. At the same time, she connected with her community: she didn't feel alone anymore. She came back to the Buddha and bowed before him and shared that she was ready to bury her son. She had understood.

If the Buddha had just said to Kisa Gotami, "Everything is impermanent; everything that's born must pass away," then that message wouldn't have been of any comfort to her at all. She had to encounter others and feel connected to the reality of impermanence in a different way—through the way of the heart.

Isn't this an exquisite example of the kind of teacher that the Buddha was?

Each one of us has encountered the teaching of the Buddha; we're very lucky people. If we ask the members of our practice community what was the first teaching that really struck a chord in them, that really pierced their heart, we'd discover that it was different for each one of us. What was your first encounter with the teaching? This is one aspect of the skillful nature of the Buddha's teaching: it speaks to us at whatever level of understanding we have, wherever we are on the path. Sometimes just a word, a sentence, or a movement is enough.

Speaking of the capacity of a small movement to teach us, I'm reminded of a German woman who came to visit Plum Village in 1998. She was Catholic and had read many of Thomas Merton's books. Some of you will recall that in the sixties Thay went to visit Thomas Merton in Gethsemani Monastery. After Thay had spent some time with the monastic community and had left Gethsemani, Thomas Merton said to the community, "Thich Nhat Hanh is a real monk. I know that he's a real monk simply by the way he opens and closes the door."

Those words of Thomas Merton had really moved this German woman, so she made plans to come to stay at Plum Village for three weeks with one intention: to observe how Thay and the community opened and closed the doors!

Who Is a Teacher?

The longer I practice, the more gratitude I have for the opportunity I've had to encounter this path. And the more my practice takes on its own momentum, the more I enjoy it. I'm in love with my practice. I also feel a lot of gratitude toward my teachers.

Buddhism places a lot of emphasis on the teacher-student relationship. I think the reason for this is that it was an oral tradition for so long, with so much transmitted by being in each other's presence, through bodily action. If you've ever been on a retreat with Thay, you've probably experienced this. Our teachers might be people, but they can also manifest in so many different ways, just like Thay taught me so many years ago: there's nothing that's not an opportunity to wake up. Our teachers are anyone who's ever offered us a word of Dharma, who's ever pierced our heart. To have the opportunity to receive teachings from a good teacher is a rare and wonderful thing. We are so fortunate.

There's a teaching in the oral tradition that I find beautiful to contemplate: our teachers are manifestations or transformation bodies of the Buddha's great compassion, who have manifested in a way that is able to bring the appropriate teaching to each one of us, so that we can open our hearts and wake up.

We've encountered the kind of teacher who can speak to our heart. Our teachers may not be perfect, but if they've offered us a single word of Dharma or a sentence that has helped us to be able to transform our heart, then they are a worthy transformation body of the Buddha, since they have awakened the seed of Dharma within us. They are kind spiritual friends; they're true friends. And, for me, that's the role of a teacher. Don't be mistaken here; true kindness is not always a box of chocolates. It'd be nice if it was, right? Kindness can sometimes be fierce if that's what's needed. But that's a story for another time.

Don't Be Fooled by the External

A teacher, a good spiritual friend, awakens our own teacher within and helps us to awaken our own Dharma body. Just like Pukkusati from this chapter, it can be sometimes challenging for us to recognize our great teachers even when they're right in front of us. If we do, we are fortunate indeed; most of the time we only recognize the great teaching later. The most challenging relationships, the most contrarian situations can be the greatest teachers of our lifetime. So don't get too caught in the externals: the great teacher in your life at this time might be your two-year-old in the middle of a temper tantrum.

A Story about Shantideva

There was a monk called Shantideva at Nalanda University, one of the great Buddhist universities of its time. Shantideva was famous in his time among the monks at Nalanda for being great at three things: eating, sleeping, and going to the bathroom! It seemed like he didn't do anything at all, and the other monks were really irritated with him. They began thinking to themselves, "We should really embarrass him so that he'll get out of here and leave us good practitioners alone."

After a lot of discussion about the best approach, they

decided to invite Shantideva to offer a teaching to the assembly. They approached him and invited him to offer a teaching, and at first he refused. But they kept begging him and begging him, and finally he agreed. But that wasn't enough for these jealous monks. They thought they'd also shame him by taking away the stairs to the podium so he wouldn't be able to climb up to it. If ever you've been to a Dharma talk in Plum Village centers, you know there's a slightly raised podium that we sit on when we offer a talk. In Nalanda, however, it was a very high podium called a "Lion's Throne," which required a ladder in order to climb up onto it.

As the story goes, Shantideva walked in and, without blinking an eye, ascended the Lion's Throne without the ladder and sat on the podium to give a talk. The talk that he gave is called the Bodhisattvavatara, The Way of the Bodhisattva, which I mentioned in the previous chapter. It is one of the most beautiful texts on bodhicitta and the practice of the paramitas in Mahayana Buddhism. I like to read a section every day because it is so beautiful and profound.

When I think of Shantideva not being frazzled, I see that our own Thay has this quality. In 2003, we happened to be in Korea on April Fool's day. All of us thought it would be really funny if we played a trick on Thay, so instead of food on Thay's breakfast tray, we placed one peanut on every small dish. We brought the tray in at breakfast time and Thay joined his palms to recite the Five Contemplations. We were all on the edge of our cushions in anticipation, waiting to see what was going to happen. After the Five Contemplations, Thay bowed, and he took the lids off each of the bowls—and his expression did not change at all. He simply picked up his chopsticks, and he ate each of the peanuts. It was a bit of a letdown actually and we brought Thay's real breakfast in straightaway. Our teachers, these kind spiritual friends, open our path for us.

The Seven Limbs of Awakening

Awakening consists of seven qualities called the Seven Factors of Awakening, sometimes called The Seven Limbs of Awakening (*sapta bodhyanga* in Sanskrit).

1. Mindfulness

The first factor of awakening, or first limb of awakening, is mindfulness, sati. Whoever begins to practice mindfulness has discovered the path of waking up already; you're already on the path. In the commentary to the Satipatthana Sutta the Buddha says, "Mindfulness, friends, is essential everywhere; it's as essential as the salt is to the curry." This is somewhat reassuring to me, since I come from a country where people are seriously unafraid of salt. My grandfather used to eat salt sandwiches. Please don't think I'm advocating that you try this. I'm simply saying that I find that the simile resonates with me. It's as essential as salt is to the curry.

When we speak of mindfulness, please remember that we're referring to the Four Establishments of Mindfulness that we encountered in an earlier chapter and that hopefully we've continued to develop. There's an interesting comment from the Buddha about mindfulness that's contained in the Dhammapada. The Buddha says, "The person who delights in mindfulness practice and abhors heedlessness dwells in the vicinity of nirvana." We're not very far from liberation, from what we are seeking: in fact we're dwelling right in its vicinity.

2. Investigation of Dharmas

The second of the Seven Factors of Awakening is investigation of Dharmas, *dhamma vicaya*. This is a quality of discernment, of cutting through surface appearances. We begin to see things as they really are; we see their component parts.

Let's take a simple example, something that we normally consider to be one entity such as "the body." If we bring the quality of investigation to the body we begin to recognize all the different parts, all the different conditions and elements that come together to make up this thing called body; or that make up this thing called happiness; or that come together to make up this thing that we call sadness or suffering.

We see things as they are; we see the cause of something, the conditions that arise together with it, and its effects. The Dharma is to be discovered by each one of us for ourselves, and not through blind faith.

Once a follower of another tradition came to hear a Dharma talk from the Buddha, and he was so impressed that he asked to take refuge then and there. His name was Upali. The Buddha actively discouraged him, saying, "You should investigate very thoroughly first." Honestly, Buddhists are not big on conversion. In fact if someone comes to us too starry-eyed, we tend to discourage it, we don't really have any missionary program. If you find something useful, you're welcome to it. If you don't find anything useful, that's okay too, we wish you well on your way.

3. Energy

The third limb of awakening, the third factor of awakening is energy or effort: *viriya*. We've discussed this practice already: the Four Right Efforts. This is also the sixth aspect of the Noble Eightfold Path, putting forth the right amount of effort, putting forth the right amount of energy. There's some energy in our practice; we're not like a zombie.

Another aspect of energy and effort is to avoid over-effort, to the point where it becomes a pushy, goal-driven mentality. I think that is often the extreme that we tend to fall into. We want to "get" something, so we push ourselves and we push others hard in our practice life. We grasp on to something, in this case, our practice, and hold it very tightly. I've often shared that for people in the West, the practice of laziness is a very important antidote to our current situation. I'm really hoping that each one of you is finding opportunities for laziness through the week, whether it's for a minute, an hour, or one day a week.

4. Joy

The fourth of the limbs of awakening is delight, *piti*. This energy of delight suffuses the whole body and mind. If we don't have this kind of experience in our practice, of delighting in and enjoying our sitting meditation, our walking meditation, our mindfulness practice, it will be hard to progress far. This element of delight manifests naturally when we have a focused attention, when we have developed the capacity to dwell with our experience. We start to enjoy things that before we didn't really pay attention to, that we used to call "neutral." Thay calls this the "non-toothache"; the non-toothache becomes delightful!

5. Ease

The fifth factor of awakening is called ease, *passaddhi*, absolute ease. *Passaddhi* is sometimes described as "royal ease." For many of us we don't really feel easeful, yet ease begins to develop as we move along in our practice, and it's described in very beautiful terms in the texts. It's described as the sensation a weary traveler would have on a hot day after walking very far and then seeing a large shady tree and coming and sitting down under the cool shade of that tree. This ease develops in our body and mind through our practice of mindfulness.

6. Concentration

The sixth factor of awakening is samadhi, concentration, or dwelling with what's there. It's an unscatteredness—our body, speech, and mind are united. It's not the kind of intellectual concentration that we get exhausted by, it's a life-giving dwelling-with, a non-struggling.

7. Equanimity

The seventh factor is equanimity, *upeksha*. This is a balance of the mind; it's not indifference. Thay sometimes translates upeksha as inclusiveness. We include all and exclude none. We're present with everything that's there.

The Seven Factors and the Four Establishments

The Seven Factors of Awakening are related to the Four Establishments of Mindfulness. When we bring our mindfulness to the four establishments—body in the body, feelings in the feelings, consciousness in consciousness, and objects of mind in the objects of mind—then these limbs of awakening naturally begin to develop. We bring in the element of investigation; we're present with the body in the body, for example. Then slowly we start to examine the different parts of our body. And as we bring that kind of awareness with the right amount of energy, delight begins to manifest; we enjoy paying attention to our breath, to our body. And there's ease. We're one with the object of our attention. We're not pushing anything away, and we're not pulling anything toward us.

The Seven Limbs of Awakening are fruits that arise from our practice of the Four Establishments of Mindfulness. We should be experiencing the development of these limbs in our consciousness as we work with the Four Establishments of Mindfulness. The seven limbs are also antidotes to the Five Hindrances that we have already explored. For example, as we get more familiar with our mind, diligence, and delight, inviting those energies, those limbs up in our consciousness can be great antidotes to dullness and drowsiness. Cultivating ease can be a great antidote to restlessness and worry, and so on.

Are you beginning to get a sense of the Buddha's teaching being like Indra's Net, that beautiful metaphor in which one jewel contains all other jewels and reflects them infinitely? The Buddha's teaching is like that. Through practicing one Dharma door we're opening the doorway to all the others; through developing the doorway that we call mindfulness, mindfulness based on the four establishments, we're opening the door for these seven limbs, these seven branches of awakening, to develop fully and beautifully in ourselves.

Reading
Nourishing Happiness

Sitting here in this moment, protected by the Sangha, my happiness is clear and alive.

What a great fortune to have been born a human, to encounter the Dharma, to be in harmony with others, and to water the Mind of Love in this beautiful garden of practice.

The energies of the Sangha and mindfulness trainings are protecting and helping me not make mistakes or be swept along in darkness by unwholesome seeds.

With kind spiritual friends, I am on the path of goodness,

illumined by the light of buddhas and bodhisattvas.

Although seeds of suffering are still in me in the form of afflictions and habit energies, mindfulness is also there, helping me touch what is most wonderful within and around me.

I can still enjoy mindfulness of the six senses: my eyes look peacefully upon the clear blue sky, my ears listen with wonder to the songs of birds, my nose smells the rich scent of sandalwood, my tongue tastes the nectar of the Dharma, my posture is upright, stable, and relaxed, and my mind is one with my body.

If there were not a World-Honored One, if there were not the wonderful Dharma, if there were not a harmonious Sangha, I would not be so fortunate to enjoy this Dharma happiness today.

My resources for practice are my own peace and joy. I vow to cultivate and nourish them with daily mindfulness. For my ancestors, family, future generations, and the whole of humanity, I vow to practice well.

In my society I know that there are countless people suffering, drowned in sensual pleasure, jealousy, and hatred.

I am determined to take care of my own mental formations, to learn the art of deep listening, and to use loving speech in order to encourage communication and understanding and to be able to accept and love.

Practicing the actions of a bodhisattva, I vow to look with eyes of love and a heart of understanding.

I vow to listen with a clear mind and ears of compassion, bringing peace and joy into the lives of others, to lighten and alleviate the suffering of living beings.

I am aware that ignorance and wrong perceptions can turn this world into a fiery hell.

I vow to walk always upon the path of transformation, producing understanding and loving kindness. I will be able to cultivate a garden of awakening.

Although there are birth, sickness, old age, and death, now that I have a path of practice, I have nothing more to fear.

It is a great happiness to be alive in the Sangha with the practice of mindfulness trainings and concentration, to live every moment in stability and freedom, to take part in the work of relieving others' suffering, the career of buddhas and bodhisattvas.

In each precious moment, I am filled with deep gratitude.[*]

---

[*] Thich Nhat Hanh, *Chanting from the Heart*.

Reading

Happiness in the Present Moment

The past has already gone, and the future has not yet come.

Let us not drown ourselves in regret for what has passed or in expectations and worry for the future.

The Buddha has said that we can be peaceful, happy, and free in this present moment.

Let us hear the Buddha's words and let go of our sadness and anxiety.

Let us come back to ourselves and establish ourselves in what is present right now.

Let us learn to recognize the conditions for happiness that are present within us and around us.

Can we hear the birds singing and the wind in the pines?

Can we see the green mountains, the white clouds, the golden moon?

The Pure Land is available in the present moment.

Every day we can enjoy ourselves in the Buddha Land.

Every mindful breath and step takes us to the Pure Land, revealing all the wonders of the Dharma body.

I am determined to let go of hurrying, competing, being busy, and disgruntled.

I shall not run after fame, power, riches, and sex because I know that this does not lead to true happiness. All it will bring me is misery and misfortune.

I shall learn to know what is sufficient, to live simply, so that I have time to live deeply every moment of my daily life, giving my body and mind a chance to heal, and to have the time to look after and protect those I have vowed to love.

I shall practice for my mind to grow in love and compassion, so that I have the ability to help beings anywhere who are drowning in craving.

I ask the buddhas everywhere to protect and guide me, to support me on my path, so that I can live in peace, joy, and freedom every day, fulfilling the deepest aspiration as your disciple whom you trust and love.*

Questions for Reflection

1. Why are you a meditator? What brought you to meditation?

2. What are some of the events, situations, people who have been teachers for you?

3. What was your first encounter with the Dharma? What woke up in you?

---

* Thich Nhat Hanh, *Chanting from the Heart.*

CHAPTER EIGHT

The Noble Eightfold Path

In late 2012, I was invited to spend some time offering retreats and enjoying time with local Sanghas throughout western Montana. I recognize that the monastic robe is an invitation for people to come up and ask and share all kinds of things. If ever you'd like to have an interesting day, follow a monastic around. One afternoon, I was asked to teach a class on Buddhism at the University of Montana, and as we were walking through the campus on the way to the classroom, a young guy stopped me and asked, "So then, what's the meaning of life?"

When he asked that question, I think he was asking it for many of us; it's a question that we all hold. What does this all mean? Is there any meaning at all? Is it all for nothing? As I reflected on the young guy's question, I started to wonder whether it might not be more helpful to reframe the question a little since it seems to me that there's a very subtle assumption underlying the question: the idea that there's a preordained ultimate purpose or an ultimate design.

This is the idea that many of us have been raised with: there is a plan all laid out, which we just somehow need to fit into. This can be a helpful construct for us to orient ourselves and to relax into the moment. But there also might be another way to view it.

Perhaps we're asking the wrong question. Perhaps the question of whether or not there's an ultimate plan all laid out, or an ultimate meaning, can prevent us from going one step further. Another way to look at this issue might be to reframe the question as: How do I live a meaningful life? How can I bring more meaning into my life?

In the Mahayana view, we take as the purpose of our life the intention to be most useful or most beneficial to others. The very intention to be of benefit to others is how we create and manifest meaning in our life not from someone or somewhere else outside of our own mind.

The Buddha's teaching is so practical and brings us right back into the core of our experience; it doesn't lead us into the realm of ideas and speculation but brings us back again and again to what's real and what's true right now. So when we hear these teachings, all the different Dharma doors we're exploring together, each of these is one of the ways that the Buddha issued an invitation for us to be able to return to our experience, to see it clearly, and to understand it more deeply than we have before.

Sometimes it seems that we hear the same teachings over and over again until we want to wash out our ears. There are some unbeneficial attitudes that can prevent the teachings from penetrating our mind stream. The main one that we suffer from, let's be real here, is an attitude of accumulating information without actually applying it to our situation.

When we consider the good qualities that develop in our mind stream, they come from two sources: those qualities that are born from insight, the flowering of understanding, and those qualities that are born from love, which we often refer to as bodhicitta, the mind of love.

Mindfulness, Concentration, and Insight Inter-Are

In an earlier chapter we considered the threefold teaching of mindfulness, concentration, and insight: their interrelationship and how they can all be considered different aspects of the same reality.

Mindfulness, concentration, and insight do not necessarily manifest in that order; they can give rise to each other. There are times that through insight, our behavior changes and we become more mindful around that situation in the future. Sometimes through being mindful, we generate insight. They all arise together.

One of the biggest tendencies we have is that we approach our practice in a goal-oriented way. Our practice can become like working through a checklist.

The Eight Aspects of the Path

When the Buddha was asked to describe his awakening and to describe the way of developing awakening, he offered the Noble Eightfold Path. It is the final answer to Buddha's question to our novice Sopaka, "What are the eight?" Many of us have heard about the Noble Eightfold Path many times already; it is one of the central teachings and practices of Buddhism. The Noble Eightfold Path is both a way to generate as well as the concrete manifestation of awakening.

If you've deeply realized what brings you joy and peace and brings others joy and peace, then insight develops and a transformation begins to occur naturally in our being. There's no struggle here. It becomes natural for you to be walking on the Noble Eightfold Path; it is the spontaneous behavior of awakening.

The entirety of the Buddha's teaching circles around the Four Noble Truths and the Noble Eightfold Path. All the myriad of teachings are elaborations of aspects of these core teachings.

1. Right Understanding

The first of the steps of the Noble Eightfold Path is Right Understanding, understanding things as they are: understanding how to apply a teaching, putting it into practice in our daily life.

Everything begins with understanding clearly. This is very subtle. Throughout our whole life, our understanding and knowledge will be growing and changing. The understanding that we have at this moment in time is not the complete, absolute truth. Understanding is not something static; it's always growing and changing, if we allow it to.

I'll never forget Thay sharing with us in 1997 that if we're doing the same thing in twenty years that we're doing today, then we've failed. In the same way that the understanding we have today will not be the same as we have tomorrow: it will be different if we're growing and we're developing on the path. This can be a little scary for some of us, since to grow in right understanding means to be willing to let go of our views, our comfortable places, and to step forward constantly into new territory.

2. Right Intention

The second aspect of the eightfold path is Right Intention, or right volition. We've explored this step in terms of right motivation: looking at the energy that moves us forward. By becoming more aware of and cognizant of the motivations, both subtle and otherwise, that we bring to different actions, different situations, different encounters, in our daily life, we become more skillful in the development of a good and wholesome motivation. I also think it is important to examine our motivations with regard to the practice: Why are we a practitioner?

3. Right Speech

The third step is Right Speech: words that are timely, words that bring joy, self-confidence, and hope, words that communicate what is true—at least to the best of our knowledge at this point and that build up rather than break down. So much of our communication is not really communication at all; it's just filling in empty space.

The Buddha described fifty-two kinds of unprofitable talk; it's not exactly wrong speech but kind of unprofitable talk. There's a whole list of different things—in fact, most of the conversations we have every day fit into at least one—and usually more like three or four—of the categories, for example, talk about politics, talk about this and that, talk about the origin of the world, talk about the gossip of the streets, the kings and rulers.

While interesting, these topics are not really conducive to developing the mind of liberation. In looking at right speech in our own lives, consider the way we use our speech energy and what we use our words for.

Our world is becoming ever more interconnected, and these days our words can travel out very far and into the future as well. This awareness can be a wonderful reminder, a great mindfulness bell for us, as we become more proactive in choosing the kind of communications we offer to others.

We're also aware of the person who we're speaking to and their situation, since the kind of communication that we offer in one situation is not very often the right style of communication for another situation or person.

This is the wonderful thing about meditation practice: it's always a path of discovery.

4. Right Action

The next step of the Noble Eightfold Path is described as Right Action. Earlier we learned a little about the bodhi-sattva Samantabhadra, the Bodhisattva of Great Action, and how to bring this energy into our lives by knowing when it's the right time to do something, knowing how we can be of benefit to ourselves and to others.

I have to say that knowing what we don't need to do is probably one of the more important aspects for us to consider and to look into. We're always busy and every single minute of our life is caught up in all of these different projects that we think are so important. In a year's time, we can't remember what they are. We seem to be very time-starved. We value busy-ness in our culture: we value those whose time is completely filled up. We don't value laziness as much as we should. I often joke with my friends that I think our culture could be completely transformed if we instituted nap time, like in some countries around the world that practice the art of taking an afternoon siesta. How would it be if here in North America, everything shut down from twelve to two in the afternoon and people had a long lunch, a little rest, and then came back to work? It's interesting to think about, isn't it?

I also think it's incredibly challenging to know what right action is in any situation. I think it's definitely true in my own case that I've looked back on situations that I've been involved in, and, even though at the time I did what I thought was the best, later on I thought, "Oh, maybe I should have done that differently," or "If I had interacted in this way, perhaps the situation would be different right now."

The best that we can do in any situation, the way to really ensure that we're coming from a place of right action, is to examine our motivation—to come back to ourselves and connect with our motivation of wanting to be of benefit, in whatever way that might manifest itself. That's the only thing we can really do but if we're able to do that, I feel pretty confident that we're engaged in right action—action that is in alignment with our deepest aspiration.

5. Right Livelihood

The next step is Right Livelihood, which is defined as livelihood that doesn't bring harm to oneself or to others. Others here are other people, animals, plants, and nature in general. Right livelihood as it's described in our mindfulness trainings is a livelihood "that helps realize our ideal of compassion and compassionate action."

Now we need to bloom where we're planted, so there's no reason why we can't become a bodhisattva right in the middle of where we are right now. There's no reason why our cubicle in the middle of a hundred other cubicles can't become a pure land, an oasis of peace. In our lives, we cannot always choose our situation, but we do have the choice how to respond. How can your work be a manifestation of your deep aspiration? That's a question for each one of us to look into.

6. Right Effort

The next of the steps of the Noble Eightfold Path is Right Effort. Right effort has been mentioned a number of times already. Does it seem to you that right effort might be something quite central to the Buddhist path? This is putting forth some effort, not in the sense of hard labor but in the sense of somebody who's cultivating their heart.

We're very lucky here in Deer Park that we have friends who come up and help us to take care of the native plants. Some plants blossom in some seasons, some blossom in others, and these friends know how to be patient and to create the good conditions for the different plants. It is the same way with our own practice life. We need to know what kind of effort to put forth in different areas of our life, not to make it into a struggle, not to have a situation where we're gritting our teeth and battling through, but rather to create the good conditions for the wonderful qualities that we all have, those qualities that are born from understanding and those qualities that are born from the mind of love, to manifest themselves in our heart and in our life.

7. Right Mindfulness

The next step is Right Mindfulness. Mindfulness can be either right mindfulness, or it can be wrong mindfulness, or not-yet-wholesome mindfulness. This is why the Buddha teaches so strongly about the importance of *yoniso manaskara* or developing appropriate attention, learning to focus our attention on that which is in alignment with our deepest aspiration. Sometimes we get caught up in and water elements of consciousness that are not helpful for the kind of qualities that we want to manifest for ourselves and for the world.

8. Right Concentration

The eighth step is Right Concentration. Concentration here is not intellectual concentration that just leaves you tired. Concentration in Buddhist meditation is a dwelling with; our mind is settling down and able to rest with one point. There's no struggle anymore. It's like sitting down under the shade of a tree on a scorching day.

The Eight Steps of the Path Inter-Are

Each of the steps of the Noble Eightfold Path contains all the others. If we look at Right Livelihood, for example, it manifests right action and right intention; it comes from right understanding, putting forth right effort. There's an element of mindfulness in there and concentration. Our body, speech, and mind are all united there. It is the same for each one of the steps of the Noble Eightfold Path.

A lot of us in our practice life have a "let's get it done" mentality. I was at a retreat and somebody made an announcement where they said, "Let's do our mindfulness and then we will go and do. . . . " I thought that was very interesting: in this person, the connection hasn't yet been made that meditation practice is not separate from daily life. As we can see in the Noble Eightfold Path, meditation practice involves all aspects of our life. This is engaged Buddhism. It's not a matter of just "doing our practice" and then getting on with our life. Rather, our life is our practice; whatever presents itself to us in this moment is our opportunity to awaken.

The point of our practice is to discover how we can make this thing in front of us something that's nourishing and healing, something that's life-giving. That is a kind of liberation already: to be able to be completely ourselves wherever we are.

Transcending Duality

In Chapter two we looked into pairs of opposites and transcending duality, the idea of "this and that." We considered this issue in terms of the Two Truths.

Are we able to perceive the interbeing nature of the pairs of opposites, just as we have experienced the interbeing nature of the steps of the path? Are we able to see how pairs of opposites actually depend on each other and contain each other? If we are able to perceive this truth, then the last duality, which is one of the most subtle dualities to overcome, is the duality of suffering and liberation (or nirvana and samsara).

As Thay has told us, if you want to transcend the world of birth and death, you need to discover it right in the middle of birth and death. Nirvana, liberation, peace, happiness, whatever word you want to use, it's not a place or a destination, rather, it is a realization that manifests right in the heart of our daily life. It's not somewhere to get to, but something that we can uncover through our practice of being able to take our daily life as the object of our contemplation.

Reading
Discourse on Taking Refuge in Oneself

I heard these words of the Buddha one time when the Lord was staying in the Mango Grove in the cool shade of the mango trees along the bank of a river in the land of Magadha. The elders Shariputra and Maudgalyayana had recently passed away. It was the full-moon day of the Uposatha Ceremony and the precepts were recited.

The Buddha spread out his sitting mat and sat facing the community.

After looking out at those gathered, he said, "As I look at our community, I see a large space left by the Venerables Shariputra and Maudgalyayana. In our Sangha, these venerables were the monks who were the most eloquent in giving Dharma talks, encouraging and instructing all the other monks, nuns, and laypeople.

"O monks, people seek two kinds of riches—material riches and the riches of the Dharma. In their search for material riches, they can go to worldly people. In their search for the riches of the Dharma, they could always go to the Venerables Shariputra and Maudgalyayana. The Tathagata is someone who is not searching for anything, whether it is material or the Dharma.

"O monks, do not be sad or anxious because Shariputra and Maudgalyayana have passed into nirvana. On large trees, filled with leaves, sumptuous fruits, and flowers, the largest branches always die or are broken first. On jeweled mountains, don't the highest peaks always erode before the smaller ones? In the Sangha of the Tathagata, the Venerables Shariputra and Maudgalyayana were the greatest students. So it is natural that these venerables would enter nirvana first. Do not give rise to feelings of sorrow or anguish. All phenomena that are born, exist, and are subject to the influence of other phenomena, in other words, all phenomena that are composite must abide by the law of impermanence and eventually cease to exist. They cannot exist eternally, without someday being destroyed. Everything we cherish and hold dear today, we will have to let go of and be separated from in the future. In not too long a time, I will also pass away.

"Therefore, I urge you to practice being an island unto yourself, knowing how to take refuge in yourself, and not taking refuge in anyone or anything else.

"Practice taking refuge in the island of the Dharma. Know how to take refuge in the Dharma, and do not take refuge in any other island or person. Meditate on the body in the body, nourishing Right Understanding and mindfulness to master and transform your cravings and anxieties. Observe the elements outside the body in the elements outside the body, nourishing Right Understanding and mindfulness to master and transform your cravings and anxieties. That is the way to take refuge in the island of self, to return to yourself in order to take refuge in the Dharma, and not to take refuge in any other island or thing."

When the bhikshus heard the Buddha offer this teaching, they were all very happy to put it into practice.[*]

---

[*] Samyukta Agama 639. See Thich Nhat Hanh, *Chanting from the Heart*.

Questions for Reflection

1) How have you created meaning and purpose in your life?

2) What activities do you find most meaningful? Which ones are difficult? Why is that, do you think?

3) What does it mean to you to be "useful" or "beneficial" to others?

CHAPTER NINE

Nine Meditations on Death

As a monastic I get to meet so many interesting people. I once had a fortune-teller tell me that I have two lifelines on my hand: one is very short and one is very long. My long lifeline is the result of being a practitioner; I've always wondered about that. In the early nineties I was working as an apprentice chef. I used to work very long hours since you can't just walk out after eight hours of work. You need to be there for as long as it takes for people to finish their meals; sometimes that can be twelve hours or more. I used to return home to sleep for a few hours and then get back to work. That's the life of a chef. It was hard, but at the same time I enjoyed every minute of it. Often I'd be on the early shift and since we always needed to be present before our superiors, I'd be in the kitchen well before six a.m. every morning. I used to spend my days off on meditation retreats. That was how I recharged myself.

Now that's an interesting juxtaposition of worlds: there was a frantic world where we were trained to do ten things at once, and another world on my days off where I was learning to focus intently on just one thing at a time, for example, my breathing. It was interesting to compare the two; there were times when I wondered how they connected. I think from this perspective that they were both necessary and balanced each other.

Because of my long hours in the kitchen, I would eat, shower, and do everything at work. I was only going home to sleep. I was living about half an hour away from where I was working in a little village called Jacobs Well. Every day I'd drive through the sugarcane fields to get to work; it was a very nice drive.

One morning I woke up early and I had the strongest urge to go to my shrine room to light a stick of incense and to recite the Three Refuges. So I went ahead and did that. On the way to work that morning, something snapped in the steering column of my car and I lost control of the vehicle. The car began swerving from side to side, eventually careening off the road and flipping over into a ditch, upside down and facing the opposite direction. I blacked out. When I came to, I was covered in broken glass. I climbed out of the car through the window that had broken, and there wasn't a scratch on me.

I often think about that day, and I consider how things could be very different right now. People say, "I know everyone needs to die, I just always thought that an exception would be made in my case." That's everyone's secret hope, let's be honest.

We are going to die. The mortality rate for humans currently hovers at around one hundred percent. Intellectually we grasp this, but we've yet to grasp it on a heart level, on a cellular level. When the Buddha was about to pass away, he looked at the gathered crowd and said, "All formations are impermanent. This is the final teaching of the Tathagata: practice diligently to liberate yourselves."

In Buddhism we speak a lot about impermanence, the ever-changing nature of all things. There was a delightful cartoon that I think might have been published in *Tricycle* magazine a number of years ago. In that cartoon they were showing a few different Buddhist hairstyles, and one of the hairstyles they featured was called "the Impermanent." I enjoyed that so much. Seriously, though, the truth of impermanence is one of the core teachings of Buddhism.

Sometimes people mistake the Buddha's teaching on impermanence as pessimistic, as kind of heavy or dark. But for me it really deepens my appreciation of what I have in this moment. This moment is a happy moment. It's never going to occur in exactly the same way it's occurring right now. How precious is that?

When I start to contemplate impermanence, it's truly awesome in the original sense of the word. This encounter, the people I'm sitting with right now, these conditions that have come together in this way to create this moment will never occur in exactly the same way again. That's really profound and amazing. And that awareness is really at the heart of what we call "the contemplation of impermanence."

What appreciation develops when I allow myself to walk through the door of impermanence? Knowing that one day I'll be separated from all I love has really helped me to say everything I need to say in this encounter now, to enjoy this moment and to not take it for granted. Everything is always changing; it's not only an idea, it's a contemplation, a concentration, a samadhi. You could call it a wake-up call for us to engage fully with our lives, to engage fully with the person in front of us, to not leave something for later so as not to have regrets.

You might think, as you read this, that I live with my head in the clouds. Well, maybe I do, but like everyone else, I've had my share of suffering in this life. If I live in the clouds contemplating the impermanent nature of life, it is because I know such knowledge nourishes my heart, even in the middle of a painful situation.

For a few years now, I have been experiencing health

challenges. Most days I experience moderate to severe pain in my body and there are days when I find it difficult to move around. This has been very challenging for me, since I like to be involved in many things. When, after a battery of tests, I was diagnosed with a complicated autoimmune disorder for which there is not currently a cure, I felt as if my own body had betrayed me. I had to rediscover my body, listen to it, and honor it. I began to embrace my situation as a teacher and to embrace my own mortality.

It's been said that Buddhists practice dying in order to live fully. As Buddhist monastics, each time we step out of our room we're supposed to leave our room in such a way that we might never return. I hope that you don't find that thought depressing. One person shared with me that it's as depressing as being somebody who sits in a dark room wearing black and smoking cigars all day. Well, that's a bit extreme! But often when we speak about death or impermanence, people have the same reaction: "Ah, that's so morbid and depressing—stop bumming me out!" But when I hear that reaction, when I see that knee-jerk response, I find myself wondering what *their* sense of happiness is based on. Is it a real joy, a grounded, embodied joy, or is it based on a denial of the facts of our existence?

There's the old saying, "There are two things that are certain in this life, death and taxes; there's no way to escape those two." In the monastic life, we sometimes joke that it's not taxes so much, it's morning meditation and oatmeal for breakfast; there's no way to get away from morning meditation and oatmeal for breakfast, so go figure.

Speaking of monastics, the Chinese word for monastic is *Chu Jia*, which is *Xuat Gia* in Vietnamese. The characters actually mean "to go out of" or "to leave home." Although this term usually applies to monastics, I think it is also helpful in terms of the practice.

What does *home* mean for you? There are so many layers of meaning. Home can be a place where we shut the world out, where we hide. Leaving home, here, then, can mean to leave behind the places we hide, the places we find our false security in order to find our true home or our true security so that we can be at ease wherever we are.

We are changing every minute, every second. As I get older—admittedly I'm not *that* old—I notice that people's greetings are changing. People used to say, "Hi, how are you?" and now more often I'm getting, "Hi, are you feeling okay?" This is a good reminder. Joking aside though, one of the big illusions we have is that we have a lot of time; that we can say or do that thing later, whenever all the conditions have come together and it's perfect.

In the mid-nineties when I was practicing in Sri Lanka I noticed that the monks there placed an emphasis on developing a strong awareness of our own mortality. I don't know if it's still being done, but novices at that time were taken to the morgue very soon after their ordination to view the dead bodies. This brought home the fact that one day we're going to pass away. Old, young, big, small—what a wake-up call.

In the place where I was staying, in the little courtyard outside of my room, there was a walking meditation path only about twenty paces long. Every day we would walk back and forth, back and forth. And at the end of my walking meditation path was a skeleton hanging on a frame. Every time I would reach the end of the path, there was this skeleton as a reminder: this will be me one day and it might be very soon. It might be today. So, knowing this, what is the most important thing for me to do in this moment?

The Nine-Point Death Meditation

I don't think many people wake up in the morning and say, "Okay, today is the day I'm going to die. I know I'm going to die this afternoon at two-fifteen." For the majority of people death comes as a complete surprise.

We practice dying or, if you prefer, we reflect on our death so that we can live fully with clear eyes.

There are a number of reflections and meditations

on impermanence and dying. One that I find particularly transformative is the Nine-Point Death Meditation. The meditation consists of three key contemplations and each one contains three reflections for a total of nine. We take the reflections and we sit with them, we walk with them, we breathe with them, and we eat with them, considering them through the lens of our own experience.

Please don't practice with these reflections as if they were mantras to say over and over again by rote. Gently invite these awarenesses to take root in your body and in your mind, and consider how they might apply in your life, in the situation you find yourself in right now.

Death Is Certain

The first contemplation is the *certainty of death*.

The first of the three reflections in this contemplation is called "*no one has ever escaped death.*"

Reflect, and through all of history, try to discover whether anyone has ever escaped death. Also consider those who are, or were, near and dear to you such as family members.

No matter how hard we try, how many supplements we take, or whether we're on a special diet, with our wrinkle creams, or even dramatic things like cryogenics or whatever, we're still going to die.

Are you any different? No matter how much we would like it to be different, am I going to be the first person that's going to live forever? Contemplate deeply this point until you find yourself at rest with the naturalness of death. This is the first reflection.

The second reflection of the first contemplation is "*my death is coming closer every moment.*" Consider that with each moment that passes by, the moment that we will transition is getting closer. It's not getting further away! As Thay shares, through mindfulness of breathing, which is really our foundational practice in the Plum Village tradition, we become aware of the births and deaths that are taking place in every moment. You are the youngest right now that you'll ever be; you're not going to get any younger than you are right now. So that's a happy thought.

The third reflection of the first contemplation is "*I don't have unlimited time to practice.*" I don't have unlimited time so I can get everything wrapped up nicely and then pass away when I am good and ready. This present opportunity is rare and precious. The awareness that time is not unlimited gives me some impetus to not leave things undone for next week or next year, to really say those things I need to say, to do those things I need to do, so that if my death happens today I won't have too many regrets. I have the opportunity right now to say the things I need to say and to do the things I need to do. What's holding me back?

The Time of Our Death Is Uncertain

The second contemplation is that "*the time of our death is uncertain.*"

The first reflection of this contemplation is that "*our life span as human beings is not fixed.*"

Earlier we mentioned about how few people got up in the morning and knew they were going to die. For most people death comes as a complete surprise. When I returned to Australia in April 2012, on our arrival in Sydney we were given a welcoming luncheon. I remember an elderly Vietnamese gentleman there who was going around and greeting everybody. We had a beautiful lunch, and then the next morning, he was hit by a car and killed. He didn't know that was going to happen, of course. Very, very few people have the luxury of a long preparation for passing away.

We can't bank on that luxury.

If you've worked in a hospice, or you've been with people who are close to death, very often fear and regret are key strong emotions that arise when someone is close to death. There is regret that we haven't done this or that, or we did not say the thing that we most needed to. The time of our death is uncertain, and yet, we always say things like, "Oh, she died so young, what a waste, that's a pity." With the awareness that our death can happen at any moment, what is it that we need to do, that we need to say, *right now*? One of these days, I guarantee, it's going to be the last morning that you wake up. That can either be a very morbid thought or it can be a very inspiring thought. It can be something that is a natural part of life and an inspiration for us to really live this day fully.

The second reflection under this contemplation is that *"there are many conditions that endanger our life."* There can be many causes of death. It doesn't necessarily need to be a big thing like a plane crash, but it can be a small thing like a virus, for example. Our life is fragile. So we contemplate just how precious, how fragile our life is. Personally, when I contemplate all the different situations that I've been through, like the one I mentioned earlier about the car accident as well as other situations, I feel how precious it is to be sitting here right now.

The third reflection is, *"Our body is also extremely fragile."* We're not superman or superwoman, we're not the man or woman of steel as much as we'd like to be, except maybe on Halloween. Our bodies are very fragile, when we look into the reality of our existence.

When I Die, What Will Be of Benefit to Me?

The third contemplation is *"at the time of my death, what is it that will be of benefit to me?"*

The first reflection is: *"my wealth and possessions, are they going to be helpful for me at the time of my death?"* I think we know the answer to that.

The second reflection is: *"my friends, my busy-ness, my status, and so on, are they going to be helpful at the moment of my passing?"* I think we also know the answer to that as well.

The final reflection is: *"how is my body going to be helpful at the time of my passing?"* Even with all of our creams, our Pilates, and our special diets, how is my body going to be helpful in that moment?

This last reflection brings us back to what kind of qualities we would like to have manifest in our mind at our passing; what is my continuation?

In Buddhist psychology, it is said that the predominant thoughts and emotions, the habitual things we take refuge in, in our daily life, the things we focus our attention on are the things that are going to become much more apparent to us when we are close to our death. They are the things that have the strongest imprint on our mind stream. When I consider this, I realize the importance of recognizing where my thoughts habitually end up and to choose to water seeds of compassion, peace, and joy.

I would like those qualities to be present in my mind during my passing.

When I take this nine-point meditation to heart, I feel moved to set my heart on the practice, to not wait until tomorrow, and to not think there's ever going to be a perfect day, when the stars are all going to magically be in alignment. That's not our human experience; it's just not going to happen. Let us do the very best that we can in the situation that we have right now: with the pain we have in our body, with the tiredness that we have, with the busyness that we have, so that we don't feel regretful later; we've lived this day wholeheartedly.

Reading

The Five Remembrances

I am of the nature to grow old.
There is no way to escape growing old.

I am of the nature to have ill health.
There is no way to escape having ill health.

I am of the nature to die.
There is no way to escape death.

All that is dear to me and everyone I love are of the nature to change.

There is no way to escape being separated from them.

I inherit the results of my actions of body, speech, and mind. My actions are my true continuation.*

Questions for Reflection

1. If I knew that I or my beloved one were going to die today, what would be the most important thing for me to say or do right now?

2. What is preventing me from doing/saying it right now?

3. What are some of the ways that I "hide" in the sense of shutting things out?

---

* Thich Nhat Hanh, *Chanting from the Heart.*

CHAPTER TEN

The Ten Recollections

Reflecting on Our Practice of the Dharma Doors

We began by creating an intention for our practice, by bringing balance to the four aspects of our practice life: the areas of study, of practice, of work, and of play. We created what we call a practice mandala to look at and use to deepen our practice.

How has that been for you? What discoveries did you make? We've looked at and practiced with Dharma doors such as the Four Nutriments. We've examined the Two Truths; the Three Roots and the Three Refuges; the Four Noble Truths, the Four Bodhisattvas, and the Four Establishments of Mindfulness; the Five Skandhas, the Five Faculties, and the Five Powers; the Six Crossings-Over; the Seven Factors of Awakening; the Noble Eightfold Path; the Nine-Point Death Meditation; and Impermanence. And in this final chapter we move into the final group of teachings, ten meditations to use throughout the day. By a very rough count I think that adds up to around seventy-six invitations to practice.

Have you been able to walk through any of these Dharma doors? It must have sometimes felt as if I've been a doorman standing at seventy-six doors holding them open for you. Have you been able to use any of these practices to shine light on aspects of your own life? It is my wish that you have found at least some of them helpful and useful.

At the end of the day it's up to you to apply the appropriate teachings in your daily life, to order and eat something from the vast menu that has been placed in front of you by the Buddha. Have you tasted any of them? If none were delicious to you, don't despair.

As I mentioned before, my grandmother used to make and decorate cakes. She was well known for her fruitcake, and she offered a slice every time we went to visit. Her whole house smelled of fruitcake—I think the smell had permeated the wallpaper and the linoleum floors. You could smell it everywhere.

As a child I hated fruitcake! I wanted anything but fruitcake! When I moved away from my family, I thought, finally, my fruitcake days are over!

Funnily enough, as an adult in my late twenties, something strange started to happen; it was really unexpected. Fruitcake would start to appear in my mind, and if I ever came across it, the smell would instantly send me back to my childhood in a very Proustian fashion. When I saw fruitcake on sale somewhere I would buy some. I even asked my aunt to send me a small one from Australia one year. Now I'm always open to a slice; I'm genuinely happy when it appears.

If some of the items on the menu that were offered in this book don't yet seem delicious for you, don't despair. Perhaps at a certain point in the future, almost by surprise, they will sneak up behind you and tap you on the shoulder, and you'll discover a treasure, a delicious dish that was there all along but for which your palate was just not quite ready.

We need to grow into some of the Dharma doors, just as we learn to like some dishes and flavors as we grow older. For some of you, the previous chapter might not have been the dish you would have wanted to order off the menu, but recollection of death and impermanence is such an important practice offered by the Buddha. He didn't teach it in order to be morbid or to be sentimental about life, but rather to help us to cultivate a quality that's called *samvega* in the Pali language. Samvega is a sense of the preciousness and the fragility of our life and the lives of other living beings, and it generates a sense of urgency about our practice and our lives—the sense of not waiting until tomorrow or that illusory day when all conditions will be perfect for us to act.

In the Poems of the Elders, "Theragatha and Therigatha," there are a number of poems that speak to this. These texts are canonical poems that have been written or were spoken and passed down by elders in the monastic lineage:

"It's too cold, too hot,
Too late," they say.
Those who neglect their work like this—
Opportunities pass them by.

But one who considers hot and cold
To be nothing more than a blade of grass;
He does his duty,
And his happiness never fails.

(Now, I love this next section:)

With my chest I'll thrust aside
The grasses, vines, and creepers,
*And devote myself to seclusion.**

Notice here that the practitioner moves forward with their heart, with their chest, with the core of their being, and not

---

* Theragatha 3.5 Matangaputta and Theragatha 1.27 Lomasakangiya. Translation by Bhikkhu Sujato with Jessica Walton. Released by Creative Commons Zero (CC0 1.0 Universal Public Domain Dedication: https://suttacentral.net/en/thag3.5 and https://suttacentral.net/en/thag1.27.

with their head. This is such an important teaching for all of us, to move forward from the core of our being, to set our heart upon liberation.

As we discussed early on, meditation is not just about paying attention, it's about developing *appropriate* attention, or yoniso manaskara. Each of the gateways that we've explored together is a contemplation, or a lens, a framework that we can use to look more deeply at our situation and understand it in ways that we never have before.

Ten Ways to Develop Your Attention

There is a very powerful practice for developing appropriate attention, which are the Ten Recollections. They are a traditional set of meditation themes that we contemplate throughout the day, which we set our heart upon. It's almost like a visualization practice. Each of these recollections plays a specific role in our practice life.

A few years ago, Thay shared that a meditation practitioner needs to be like an artist—notice he didn't say "like a paint-by-numbers person"; the artwork we produce is going to look a little bit different for each one of us. If we ask Van Gogh, Picasso, and Vermeer, for example, to paint the same scene, they would all offer very different paintings, right?

The Ten Recollections are like artist's tools, or if you're a cook like me, perhaps you could say they're like spices. You need to know when and how to use each one. By way of example, I think that unless you were in dire need of an extra special breakfast experience, you probably wouldn't want a tablespoon of cayenne pepper in your oatmeal. (Or maybe you would, I don't know.)

Some of the Ten Recollections are practices and some are objects of contemplation. The first six of the Ten Recollections help to cultivate a sense of delight and confidence, *pasada* in the Pali language. Delight and confidence help lead us into meditation and concentration; they are supportive factors for the element of samadhi to develop. It is extremely rare for a fruitful meditative concentration to develop without the supporting factor of pasada.

The remaining recollections cultivate a sense of our own worthiness on the path, a sense of our own good qualities. In Buddhist psychology the acknowledgment and recognition of our own innate goodness is essential.

The first three recollections are of the Buddha, the Dharma, and the Sangha. There are beautiful texts about the Triple Gem, and traditionally there are verses of recollection that extol the qualities of the refuges that we recite every day. When we work with the Ten Recollections, for example, the recollection of the Buddha, the object of our attention and contemplation, are the qualities manifested in the World-Honored One, and the qualities that he awakened in others.

We begin to recognize these qualities within ourselves, and in those we encounter in our daily life. The presence of the Buddha, of the energy of awakening, becomes something very real and tangible for us. Or you can say the presence of the awakened mind becomes something very real and tangible for us.

It's so helpful to call to mind the qualities of great compassion and wisdom that are embodied in the person of the Buddha. We might like to remember his great skillfulness as a teacher, as we recall in the story of Kisa Gotami, and the qualities he embodied of the Dharma and the Sangha. One traditional way to really allow these recollections to infuse our consciousness is to read and reflect on the recollection verses daily.

When I was in Sri Lanka, we would recite the verses of recollection in the Pali language every day. If we read them regularly, then they become a part of us. A word or a phrase will pop up and be present in our mind at various points throughout the day.

1. Recollection of the Buddha

As I mentioned earlier, there are some lovely texts on the

Three Jewels. One of the most beautiful texts is in the Anguttara Nikaya. A monk called Mahanama approached the Buddha and asked him, "How should we dwell?" The Buddha responds beautifully, answering that we should dwell in the recollections whether walking, standing, sitting, or lying down, whether we are busy at work or at home with our house filled with children.

Now please remember back to when we discussed that samadhi, or concentration, in Buddhist meditation is a "dwelling with," a dwelling with our meditation object. When we hear in this text about dwelling places, this is what Mahanama is referring to, the dwelling place of our attention. This is what is meant by the question, "By means of which dwelling place should we live?"

The recollections are not just practices to be done when we sit down to meditate, but practices to develop awareness throughout our daily life. As we develop the first recollection, we begin to recognize and recall these qualities in our mind. We see how we manifest these qualities in our daily life and how they present themselves to us.

This is a beautiful way for us to be able to be in contact with the energy of the awakened mind as it presents itself to us in each moment of our daily life.

2. Recollection of the Dharma

Then we move on to the recollection of the Dharma, which goes as follows: The Dharma is well proclaimed by the Blessed One, is to be realized here and now, it is immediately useful and effective, inviting all to come and see directly. *

3. Recollection of the Sangha

The third recollection is about the Sangha. When we bring to mind the qualities of the Sangha, the energies of joy, delight, and confidence will manifest in our mind, allowing us to develop concentration.

We turn these qualities over in our minds; they're not just things to recite, but to recite and reflect upon. Do we find these qualities manifesting in the Buddha? Do we see these qualities manifesting in the Dharma? Do we experience these qualities when we're in contact with the Sangha? We recognize the presence of our refuge in each moment of our daily life. Buddhism is not about what we do on Sundays, or on Days of Mindfulness, or on the cushion, but about how we engage with every moment. Dwelling in the recollection of the Three Gems, these first three recollections, which is such an important practice in the Buddhist world, has a profound effect on our mind.

---

* Thich Nhat Hanh, *Chanting from the Heart*, "The Four Recollections."

There's a story from the Sutta Nipata about a monk who was dwelling in the forest. The text tells us that unfortunately this monk spent his day "thinking evil and unskillful thoughts, thoughts of ill will, thoughts of doing harm." The poor man! Now, in traditional Buddhist cosmology, there are divine beings, and we see these divine beings, or *devas*, mentioned in some of the texts like the Discourse on Happiness, "Many divine beings and humans are eager to know what is the greatest happiness?"

It's up to our own discernment and reflection whether we understand the reference to divine beings as one of the Buddha's skillful means to speak in a way that was culturally appropriate to the time, or whether we want to take it on faith, that there are divine beings or spirits or whatever; that's up to you.

The story goes that there was a deva inhabiting the forest thicket, and who felt a lot of sympathy for the monk. One of the things that's often mentioned in the texts is that when we perform meritorious actions—thinking thoughts of loving kindness, and trying to benefit each other, and protecting the Earth, and also dedicating our meritorious actions, then the devas—and indeed the whole of nature—rejoice together with us, and become sympathetic allies. Dedicating the merit or rejoicing in the merit of others is the lazy person's way to develop merit and virtue and it's also a wonderful way to minimize our critical and judging minds.

Seeing that this monk was not practicing well, the deva felt sympathy for him. Desiring to bring him to his senses, she approached him and addressed him with the following verse: "From inappropriate attention, you are being chewed up by your thoughts."

It's pretty powerful stuff, isn't it? "You're being chewed up by your thoughts." I know that there have been times in my life when I've felt completely chewed up by my thoughts.

She then goes on to invite him to let go of what is no longer serving and to contemplate appropriately, keeping his mind on the Buddha, the Dharma, and the Sangha, as well as his own good qualities, which will help him to be "saturated with joy." How beautiful is that phrase, "saturated with joy." I love it. Every cell of our body is imbued with joy and delight in the practice. This is the fruit of the first three recollections. When we reflect on the beautiful qualities of the Buddha; the Dharma that is beautiful in the beginning, beautiful in the middle, and beautiful at the end; the Sangha of practitioners, who are practicing uprightly, who are offering teachings, who are present for us, whether in monastic form or in lay form, who are a little bit everywhere, then feelings of fear, isolation, separation, begin to melt away and we become saturated in joy.

4. Recollection of Your Own Virtue

The fourth recollection is recollection of virtue, recalling our meritorious actions. I think it is incredibly pertinent for us in the current day, and it's something that we do not do enough. I can't stress this more strongly—we do not do this fourth recollection often enough. It's almost as if we have an aversion to it. It basically means recollecting, bringing to mind, all of our own good qualities, all of the beautiful seeds that we have in our own consciousness, the beautiful qualities that we offer out to others: qualities of joy, compassion, and forgiveness.

I think we need this medicine most of all. So many of us feel that we're just not quite good enough. And so the fourth recollection is a powerful way for us to be able to be in contact with our own innate goodness, the fact that we have this wonderful seed of awakening, a deeply compassionate heart within us.

There's a little text in the Pali canon that shares about the recollection of virtue from the Anguttara Nikaya. It reminds us that recollection of our good qualities gives rise to joy, ease, and meditative concentration.

Just as a little aside here, this is a special kind of pleasure, pasada, meditative delight. It's not necessarily the pleasure that we might experience while eating a gelato or something like that, but a different kind of pleasure altogether.

In the same text, we are invited to develop this recollection in every position of the body, while we are busy and in our home full of children.

Our home might not be crowded with children, but it can be crowded with projects, with expectations, all kinds of other things. When we recollect our own virtues we also see the connection between our own good qualities and the qualities of the Awakened One, of the Buddha. We see that we too have seeds of compassion and seeds of understanding. We too have the capacity to wake up.

We develop not only a sense of confidence in the Buddha that we think is outside of ourselves, somewhere else, but we recognize the qualities that we call "Buddha" within ourselves. We develop confidence right where we are at this moment.

5. Recollection of Generosity

The next recollection is recollection of generosity. Earlier, we shared about the different kinds of gifts: the gift of material things, the gift of the Dharma, and the gift of non-fear.

In this recollection, we bring to our mind all of the different gifts and supportive conditions we receive from others. We also reflect on the gifts and supportive conditions we offer to others. And as we develop this kind of awareness, as we dwell in awareness of generosity, a mind of gratitude, of not taking things for granted, arises.

This quality of appreciation for what's being offered to us, and appreciation for the chance to offer something back, is such an important quality on the path.

If we're working with this recollection, some questions we may find helpful are, "What have I received from the kindness of others today?" "In what ways have people reached out to me?" or, "In what ways have supportive conditions become present for me this day?"

A second area of reflection might be, "In what ways have I reached out to others?" "In what ways have I been a supportive condition, or tried to create supportive conditions, for others?"

A third area might be, "Are there areas or situations or times today that I notice myself holding back, that I wanted to reach out, but I didn't; why might that be?" *

6. Recollection of the Fruits of Virtuous Action

The next recollection is traditionally described as recollection of the devas, the divine beings. A modern interpretation might be to reflect on the fruits of virtuous action. When

---

* For more elucidation of this beautiful practice, see Gregg Krech, *Naikan: Gratitude, Grace, and the Japanese Art of Self-Reflection* (Berkeley, CA: Stone Bridge Press, 2001).

we read in the traditional texts about the devas, we see that they are described as being in their position as divine beings thanks to their practice of meritorious actions, developing the crossings-over of generosity, of wisdom, of mindfulness trainings. So it can be very helpful, with this recollection, to consider the benefits of meritorious action, to consider how it would be to allow ourselves to be moved, to be inspired by the good seeds in our consciousness—what effects would they have for our own life and the lives of those around us?

This is the kind of atmosphere, the kind of intention that we're developing in this recollection, the recollection of the devas.

7. Recollection of Breathing

The next recollection is mindfulness of in- and out-breathing; *anapanasati*. At this point we see the transition in the recollections between practices that are more mental and actual physical practices. Mindfulness, sati, can also be translated as recollection. So recollection of our breathing is another one of the Ten Recollections. And we've learned a lot now about mindfulness of breathing—the most fundamental practice in our Plum Village tradition.

8. Recollection of Death

The next recollection, funnily enough, is the recollection that we began to practice in the last chapter: mindfulness of death, the Nine-Point Death Meditation. This is a very powerful practice. So since we explored it in depth in the previous chapter I won't go into any more explanation now, except to tap you in a friendly way on the shoulder in the hope that you might be practicing it!

9. Recollection of Mindfulness
   Immersed in the Body

This recollection could almost be described as a companion to the earlier recollection on the in-and out-breath. We practice to root our mindfulness firmly in our body and its sensations. As we work with this recollection, we gain a sense of the impermanent nature of our body. It can be helpful to contemplate the thirty-two parts of your body traditionally described in the Khuddakapatha.* "There are in this body: hairs of the head, body hairs, nails, teeth, skin; flesh, sinews, bones, bone-marrow, kidneys; heart, liver, pleura, spleen, lungs; intestines, mesentery, undigested food, excrement; bile, phlegm, pus, blood, sweat, fat; tears, grease, spit, mucus, synovial fluid, urine; and the brain in the head."

---

* Khuddakapatha 3. Translated by Bhikkhu Anandajoti: https://suttacentral.
  net/en/kp3

10. Recollection of Stilling

The final recollection is recollection of physical and mental stillness: we recall how it feels when all of the different energies that pull us and push us, our worries, are completely calmed and we practice to notice those moments of pure balance and delight, of being fully present, as they occur in our meditation and in our daily lives.

Practicing Daily Remembrance

These recollections are all very much related to each other but we don't try necessarily to do them all at once, just as, as much as we would wish it to be otherwise, we can't eat every single dish on the smorgasbord at once. You could try but it wouldn't be so pleasant; they would all mix together.

Perhaps choose one day when throughout the day we call to our mind the qualities of the Awakened One. And then the next day, we spend time dwelling on the qualities of the Dharma, reflecting on the qualities of the Sangha, and so on in a sequential, ordered way. And then we come back to the beginning, and we go through them again and again. Every time I read the text and I engage in the practice of the Ten Recollections, I discover something new; a different area of my heart is touched.

Questions for Reflection

1. Looking at your practice plan—your mandala of study, practice, work, and play that you created in the first chapter—how have you done? Were you able to continue on with all of your suggestions, or did you find that you needed to adjust along the way?

2. Were there practices or topics that you found especially challenging?

3. Reflecting over the whole book, which "dishes" did you find really delicious? Which elements were you were ready for?

4. What will you be taking away, and what are you looking forward to focusing on in the coming months? How will this experience continue to live on in you?

I wish each and every one of you, wherever you may be, the very best in your practice. And I hope that you got some benefit from this book, however big or little. If a single sentence has been helpful out of the thousands here, then I will be happy and content.

I hope there were a couple of dishes that you could eat—or at least taste one or two spoonfuls!

Recommended Reading

Krech, Gregg. *Naikan: Gratitude, Grace, and the Japanese Art of Self-Reflection*. Berkeley, California: Stone Bridge Press, 2001.

Red Pine. *The Heart Sutra*. Berkeley, California: Counterpoint Press, 2005.

Thich Nhat Hanh. *Cultivating the Mind of Love*. Berkeley, California: Parallax Press, 2008.

————. *Understanding Our Mind: 50 Verses on Buddhist Psychology*. Berkeley, California: Parallax Press, 2006.

————. *The Heart of the Buddha's Teaching*. New York, NY: Broadway Books (Crown Publishing), 1999.

Woodward, F. L. *Some Sayings of the Buddha*. New Delhi, India: Asian Educational Services, 2002.

Acknowledgments

There are so many hands and hearts who have held myself and this book in their loving awareness—it would never have happened without you! Come to think of it, I would never have happened without you.

To my large, loud, extended family and friends for always being there through thick and, more often, thin . . . there's never been a dull moment but I don't want to get ahead of myself—those are stories for my second book. Consider yourself warned!

To the monastic and lay family of Deer Park Monastery—words cannot express my gratitude for the time, space, love—and vegan red velvet cupcakes—you provided.

I'm grateful to Azara Turaki for being the person who requested this series of teachings: may all merit and blessing be yours.

Rachel and all at Parallax Press as well as Ron Forster and Laura Hunter: I hope one day to have your energy and dedication.

Special mention, as always, to the inimitable Brother Phap Dung and Janus Staffe. Who would have thought I would be so lucky as to know you? Hope the feeling goes both ways!

To my beloved soul sister Afrodeity Stone and to Dr. Changok Kim—you have quite literally kept me alive, thank you.

A deep bow to the huldufolk: the eyes may not always see, but the heart truly knows.

And to you who have bravely picked up this book: may it be a blessing on your way.

About the Author

Originally from Australia, Brother Phap Hai is a senior student of Zen Master Thich Nhat Hanh. He received Lamp Transmission from Zen Master Thich Nhat Hanh in January 2003 and became an authorized Dharma Teacher. Prior to becoming a monk, he trained as a chef. Brother Phap Hai is known for his ability to convey complex teachings in an accessible and humorous manner and leads retreats and workshops throughout the United States, Canada, South America, Australia, and Asia. He currently resides at Deer Park Monastery, in California, where he breathes, walks, and smiles on a regular basis.

Related Titles

Awakening Joy   James Baraz
and Shoshana Alexander

Breathe, You Are Alive!   Thich Nhat Hanh

Happiness   Thich Nhat Hanh

Learning True Love   Sr. Chan Khong

Mindfulness as Medicine   Sr. Dang Nghiem

Not Quite Nirvana   Rachel Neumann

Pass It On   Joanna Macy

Transformation and Healing   Thich Nhat Hanh

Understanding Our Mind   Thich Nhat Hanh

World as Lover World as Self   Joanna Macy

**PARALLAX
PRESS**

Parallax Press is a nonprofit publisher, founded and inspired by Zen Master Thich Nhat Hanh. We publish books on mindfulness in daily life and are committed to making these teachings accessible to everyone and preserving them for future generations. We do this work to alleviate suffering and contribute to a more just and joyful world.

For a copy of the catalog, please contact:

Parallax Press
P.O. Box 7355
Berkeley, CA 94707
(510) 525-0101
parallax.org

planting seeds of Compassion

**If this book was helpful to you, please consider joining
the Thich Nhat Hanh Continuation Fund today.**

Your monthly gift will help more people discover mindfulness,
and loving speech, which will reduce suffering in our world.

**To join today, make a one-time gift, or learn more, go to:
www.ThichNhatHanhFoundation.org.**

Or copy this form & send it to:
Thich Nhat Hanh Continuation and Legacy Foundation
2499 Melru Lane, Escondido, CA USA 92026

❐ Yes! I'll support Thich Nhat Hanh's work to increase mindfulness.
I'll donate a monthly gift of:

❐ $10   ❐ $30 ($1 a day)   ❐ $50*   ❐ $100   ❐ $___Other

*Your monthly gift of $50 or more earns you a free subscription to *The
Mindfulness Bell*, a journal of the art of mindful living (US/Canada only).

❐ Please debit my bank account each month. I've enclosed a blank check
marked "VOID."

❐ Please charge my credit card each month.

Your Name(s)_____
Name on Card/Account_____
Credit Card No._____ Exp. Date _____
Address_____
City_____ State/Prov___ Zip/Postal_____
Country___ Email_____

www.ThichNhatHanhFoundation.org
info@ThichNhatHanhFoundation.org

**PARALLAX
PRESS**

Parallax Press, a nonprofit organization, publishes books on engaged Buddhism and the practice of mindfulness by Thich Nhat Hanh and other authors. All of Thich Nhat Hanh's work is available at our online store and in our free catalog. For a copy of the catalog, please contact:

Parallax Press
P.O. Box 7355
Berkeley, CA 94707
Tel: (510) 540-6411
parallax.org

Monastics and laypeople practice the art of mindful living in the tradition of Thich Nhat Hanh at retreat communities worldwide. To reach any of these communities, or for information about individuals and families joining for a practice period, please contact:

Plum Village
13 Martineau
33580 Dieulivol, France
plumvillage.org

Blue Cliff Monastery
3 Mindfulness Road
Pine Bush, NY 12566
bluecliffmonastery.org

Magnolia Grove Monastery
123 Towles Rd.
Batesville, MS 38606
magnoliagrovemonastery.org

Deer Park Monastery
2499 Melru Lane
Escondido, CA 92026
deerparkmonastery.org

The Mindfulness Bell, a journal of the art of mindful living in the tradition of Thich Nhat Hanh, is published three times a year by Plum Village. To subscribe or to see the worldwide directory of Sanghas, visit **mindfulnessbell.org**.